COLONIAL LIVING

COLONIAL LIVING

written and illustrated by E D W I N   T U N I S

THOMAS Y. CROWELL COMPANY
New York

Books by Edwin Tunis

CHIPMUNKS ON THE DOORSTEP

COLONIAL CRAFTSMEN

COLONIAL LIVING

FRONTIER LIVING

INDIANS

OARS, SAILS AND STEAM

SHAW'S FORTUNE

THE TAVERN AT THE FERRY

WEAPONS

WHEELS

THE YOUNG UNITED STATES

L.C. Card 75-29611
ISBN 0-690-01063-X

This book is for

HELEN AND BILL CHITTICK

who seem likely to enjoy it

more than most

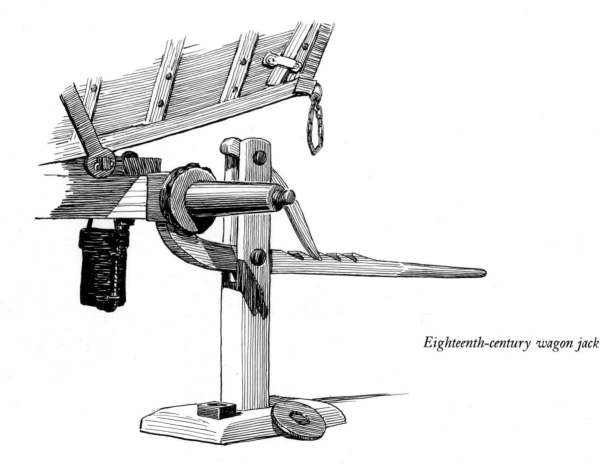

Eighteenth-century wagon jack

PREFACE

THIS IS AN ATTEMPT to describe, in one volume, the ways of pioneer life in North America during the years that can truthfully be called Colonial: 1564 to, say, 1770. It is necessarily a simplified account. Its phases have been minutely examined in scholarly books that too often are left standing on library shelves. Here are the small, common things of Colonial existence. This isn't history; it is rather a description of the stage set for history, and of the costumes and properties of the actors, spear carriers as well as the leads.

In showing things in use, as they were made to be used, and against their proper backgrounds, it has seemed justifiable to take some liberties, even at the risk of minor inaccuracies. A few of the illustrations show buildings of which no actual picture exists; however, they have been drawn with due respect to what *is* known about them, bolstered by reasonable probability, as suggested by European structures and practices of the time.

Thanks are given to collectors and antiquarians for the immeasurable help their studies have been, and apologies are offered to them for the slight treatment their specialties have received. There are antiques here, but this isn't a book about antiques. Incidentally, it isn't purposely quaint, or picturesque, either. The illustrations avoid sagging roofs and the "artistic" marks of age. Everything was new once.

The principal goal has been to get Colonial life into perspective by a general survey; a secondary object: to restore the seventeenth century to that perspective. For too many of us, American life jumps at one leap from Plymouth to Williamsburg.

It's hoped that some picture of our forebears themselves emerges from their ways of life. They weren't always admirable—neither, one fears, are their descendants—but they had qualities of fortitude and of "rugged individualism" that are worth remembering.

Acknowledgments

IN THIS TIME of jets and atoms, the simple ways of the settlers seem strange and ancient, but we are closer to them than we realize. Their homely phrases are daily on our lips, and there are living men who practice, or have practiced, crafts that persist almost unchanged from Colonial days. The help of a few such men has been invaluable in clarifying details.

Many and diverse people have given aid to this job and have gone to great trouble to do so. Special books have been obtained; one through a whole chain of people, living miles apart. Busy museum directors have given their time and interest and have verified facts.

My beholden thanks, then, are given to: Mr. Louis Bolander, Librarian, the United States Naval Academy; Mr. Halbert Nelson Cox; Mr. John Cummings, Curator, The Bucks County Historical Society Museum; Lt. Col. Paul H. Downing; Mr. Carl W. Drepperd, Curator, the Pennsylvania Farm Museum of Landis Valley; Mr. Douglas A. Fisher; Mr. James W. Foster, Director, the Maryland Historical Society; Mr. Alan Gent; Mr. John Gould; Mr. J. Paul Hudson, Curator, the National Park Service Museum at Jamestown; Mr. Albert C. Manucy, the National Park Service Historian at Castillo de San Marcos, St. Augustine; Miss Hope Henderson McGee; Mr. Arthur Pierce Middleton, Research Director, Colonial Williamsburg; Miss Mabel A. Parmenter, Curator, the South Natick Historical Museum; Mr. Arthur Perry; Dr. Winthrop M. Phelps; Com. and Mrs. Richard E. Townsend; and Mr. C. M. Watkins, Assistant Curator of Cultural History, the United States National Museum. All of these kind people are absolved from responsibility for the accuracy of this book.

Above all and as always, I am grateful to Lib, my indispensable wife, for long, long hours of hard work.   E. T.

CONTENTS

ILLUSTRATIONS

The Sixteenth and
Seventeenth Centuries

THE BEACHHEADS

BEACHHEADS, because they were the first toe holds seized by white men along the edge of North America. No modern amphibious force advancing on an enemy-defended coast ever approached more warily than did those settlers toward the silent shore of the red man's continent.

At Jamestown the landing party was greeted by a flight of arrows from out of the silence; the Indians of those parts had met whites before and had been misused by them. But for the most part the Indians, having no idea of what was coming, were friendly enough, though temperamental. There were only a few hundred thousand of them in all of North America and the idea of sharing their hunting grounds with a few more mouths didn't trouble them. Of the ownership of land and its transfer by purchase, they hadn't the least comprehension. They accepted the trinkets and tools offered in payment for their land as mere gifts of good will, or as tribute, and they usually came back at intervals for more. It wasn't until the seventeenth century was well along that they began to realize that their hunting grounds were being taken from them and, too late, they got tough.

Early in the sixteen-hundreds there were shacks, used as temporary shelters by European fishermen, along the coasts of Maine and Nova Scotia; quite possibly the Norsemen paused a while, much earlier, on Cape Cod, but there was nothing of permanence, perhaps no intention of permanence, in these camps.

The first record of white men coming to North America with the idea of staying is of some French Huguenots in 1564. They built a triangular palisade, which they named Fort Caroline, on an island in the St. Johns River, in Florida. Even the island itself has washed away now.

St. Augustine as it may have looked about 1585

ST. AUGUSTINE

A YEAR LATER the Spanish, under Pedro Menéndez de Avilés, started St. Augustine a few miles south of Fort Caroline. Though St. Augustine was sacked and burnt from time to time, it managed to survive as the first permanent European settlement north of Mexico. It was never much more than a military camp, the northernmost of the chain of forts that protected shipping in the Caribbean. The Spanish were well settled in the islands and St. Augustine was to them a frontier post, only a couple of days' sail from civilization.

ROANOKE

ST. AUGUSTINE was close to its supply base in Cuba. The first English beachhead, Roanoke Island, was different. In the Sound, just behind the deadly Outer Banks of North Carolina, it lay a long, bitter way from England and Sir Walter Raleigh spent a fortune failing to set up an "English Nation" there. Perhaps he might have succeeded if he and all the folks at home hadn't had to give their full attention to fending off the Spanish Armada, just when the Roanoke colony needed supplies and protection.

The settlers there built a little earth fort about fifty feet square with bastions at its corners. Time all but obliterated it, but archaeological sleuthing found its outlines, and its small ramparts and surrounding ditch have been put back as they were. A few buttons and buckles and corroded tools have been dug up at the site. As is well known, when relief ships finally reached Roanoke, they found nothing and nobody—only the word, "croatan," carved into a post.

The English heard the Indians say something like *wingan-da-coa* and assumed it was the native name of the country. Actually it meant "you wear pretty clothes." The leaders at Roanoke wore the full panoply of armor and bombast-padded breeches, of steel morions and flat "city" caps. The rank and file wore full breeches, called slops, tied at the knee, and a pointed doublet with welted shoulders and separate sleeves tied on. Not a few would wear a gold ring in one ear. In place of the starched ruff of the gentry (which must have gone pretty limp on Roanoke Island) the commoners wore wide collars attached to their shirts.

There were women along. They wore doublets, too, and long skirts (which they called petticoats), and shoes with thick cork soles, called chopines. About their necks was a high collar or a small ruff, and on their heads a close-fitting cap which completely covered their hair.

At Jamestown a few years later, where there were only men at first, the clothes of the "commonalty" were exactly the same as at Roanoke, give or take a little for personal taste. The more pretentious clothes hadn't changed too much either: a hat with a crown and a feather instead of the flat cap; less padding in the breeches, or sometimes ballooning Dutch breeches tied at the knee,

with no padding at all. Armor was worn and needed. It wasn't much good against bullets but it would turn an Indian arrow.

Though there are in existence some remarkably good water colors of Indians and animals made by John White, who was in charge of the Roanoke colony and who was the grandfather of Virginia Dare, the first child of English blood known to have been born in America, they show nothing of life in the colony or of any of the dwellings that were built there. We can be reasonably sure that these were not such logs cabins as have since been set about the place by the hands of modern restorers.

Wattle-and-daub cabins supported on "crotchets"

JAMESTOWN

PROBABLY the shelters at Roanoke and the first "cabbins" that were built at Jamestown when the tents rotted were much alike: a thatched roof supported on forked posts, with walls of wattle-and-daub. These were made by filling in the wall space with vertical stakes set a few inches apart, then weaving willow or hazel branches in and out horizontally and plastering both sides of the fabric with mud. Such structures didn't have to be invented on the spot; very poor people all over Europe had been living in them for centuries.

These Virginia huts probably had no chimneys but simply a hole in the roof through which smoke might find its way out, as it did from the wigwams of the Indians. It seems likely that so shiftless a lot as the first settlers at Jamestown wouldn't bother with anything that added any work. They wouldn't hunt, or fish, or plant; they were looking for gold. They didn't bother to dig a well, but took their water from the James River, at the ebb tide when the water was least salt.

Since no gold turned up it was deemed neces-

Riving clapboards.
The inset shows the froe and the splitting
needed to produce the first clapboard

sawn to the wedge shape which makes them over-lap readily. In the seventeenth century clapboards were only about four feet long and they were shaped by being split, or riven, from a log that long and usually about ten inches thick. An implement called a froe was used for the job. It was really a wide wedge: a straight, heavy blade, at one end of which a handle was hafted, making a right angle with the spine of the blade. A log was stood on end, against a prop, the edge of the froe was held across its upper end, and the thick spine of the blade was pounded with a club until the log was halved. The halves were then split repeatedly until the log was reduced to a pile of (barring accidents) two dozen boards, each about five-eighths of an inch thick on one edge and about nothing on the other. A ten-inch-diameter log gave you roughly five-inch clapboards. On a building these were lapped an inch or so to keep out the weather. Such clapboards were widely used in this country, well into the nineteenth century.

sary to ship *something* home to the London Company who were the sponsors of the venture. So John Smith put everybody to splitting clapboards, to their vast distaste. These were not to cover their own dwellings; they were strictly for export.

Modern clapboards are full-length lumber,

PLYMOUTH

THE FIRST PROBLEM of settlers, once they had their feet on land, was temporary shelter. At Plymouth, at New Amsterdam, and much later at Philadelphia, this took the form of a hole in the ground. It was given a bark-covered roof supported on poles. Sometimes the pit was dug into a hillside and had a front wall and partial side walls of sod or bark. As the colonies grew these earth houses moved inland; they were usually the first dwelling in any new clearing until the frontiersmen learned to build log cabins. Once they had themselves organized, the coastal settlers put up small, timber cottages and abandoned their "smoky homes" with relief.

These Plymouth settlers wore simple clothes, but there is no ground whatever for the unshakeable assumption that they all wore black and white. They tended much more to wear browns, tans, and rusty reds. They wouldn't have worn extreme clothes, even if they could have afforded them, but aside from that they dressed as their social class did in England: low shoes tied with

latchets (this was before buckles), seldom boots (they were too costly); knitted wool or woven cloth stockings; full breeches, usually of leather; a plain leather jerkin; a white linen shirt with the collar outside; shoulder-length hair, and a soft cap, or a wide-brimmed hat with a low, round crown.

The women may have worn high-crowned hats; there seems to be a tradition that they did. If so, a hood, or "head rail," was probably worn beneath the hat, with perhaps a close-fitting white coif under the hood. Over a simple doublet, they almost all wore a white neckcloth, and below the doublet a full skirt, hanging naturally and not spread wide on a farthingale as worn by grand ladies in England. Any of these women would probably have been embarrassed if she had been seen in public without an apron.

The Pilgrims of Plymouth were poor men, largely illiterate. Most of them were minor artisans who had always lived in towns. They knew nothing of how to organize an expedition to a wild country and nothing of how to survive when they

Bark-roofed dugout at Plymouth

had reached it. They had intended to go to Virginia, but the *Mayflower's* skipper made a miscalculation, which he refused to rectify, and landed them in a far more rigorous climate. He did stand by in the harbor until spring, so the ship could be used as a base while the hovels were being built.

These people were no good at hunting; most of them had never fired a gun or a crossbow. They had counted on fishing and there were plenty of fish, but the hooks they had were all too big for any fish they could reach in the bay. The scanty supplies of food were soon gone; of 102 who landed only 50 lived out the winter; four women survived.

There was no lack of fortitude. The remnant allowed the *Mayflower* to go home in the spring without them! The end would have been swift but for two Indians, Samoset and "Squanto." Both of them spoke some English. "Squanto" was not the sole survivor of a South Shore tribe, as most history books say he was. Mr. John Gould has reestablished his identity as Tisquantum, one of five Pemaquid Indians from Maine kidnapped and taken to England some fifteen years earlier.

Tisquantum showed the colonists how to hunt

The Plymouth settlers planting corn

and how to catch fish. He taught them how to plant Indian corn and presumably procured the seed for them. They planted in Indian fashion, girdling the trees to kill them, so the sun could shine through, and then sticking the seed into the ground without plowing. A fish was put into each hill as fertilizer. Squash, which, like the corn, was new to the settlers, was planted among the corn, and bean vines climbed the cornstalks. The importance of Indian corn to the settlers of America cannot be overestimated.

It was to celebrate the harvest of this planting that the famous first Thanksgiving dinner was held, though the spirit of the occasion must have been somewhat dampened by the arrival of thirty new settlers, who naturally had no food with them. Sixty-five more arrived in the spring of 1622, and everybody starved all summer while the crops were growing. That they survived at all must be credited to the New England clam which Tisquantum had shown them how to find at low tide.

NEW AMSTERDAM

THE DUTCH established their trading post on Manhattan Island in 1623, but some of their countrymen had been squatting there for ten years before that and the outpost at Albany had been established in 1614. The new settlers built huts, too, at first, probably all dugouts. Dugouts were built by up-country settlers as late as 1650.

Since the Hollanders had all come over for the fur trade with the Indians and originally had no plans for agriculture, and since they also were hearty eaters, they brought plenty of food with them. Most of them seem to have had no notion of staying permanently; the idea was to make a pile of guilders and get out. The descendants of some of them are still on the island and it is still the trading post it never ceased to be.

Puritan wigwams

MASSACHUSETTS BAY

IN 1630 WHEN the Puritans arrived in Massachusetts Bay, 900 strong, they came better equipped and better organized than either the Virginians or the Pilgrims had been. Their leaders were prosperous farmers and they were socially, economically, and intellectually a cut above the

Plymouth settlers. Not that all of the large vanguard that landed at Salem were of this class, of course, or even were all Puritans, but the leaders were. They had the Bible under one arm and their royal charter under the other. The Bible was always in evidence but the charter was kept so carefully concealed that in time some people began to think it was a myth. It wasn't. The English authorities didn't expect the Puritans to bring their charter with them; the correct thing to do was to leave it in London and to submit meekly to government from there. John Winthrop and John Endicott were of tougher fiber than that; they did their own governing on the spot.

These people too had need of quick shelter, but they didn't go underground. They built copies of the Indians' lodges, adding chimneys instead of putting up with smoke-holes. The chimneys, built of sticks and clay, were neither durable nor safe and frequently caught fire. The lodges were not at all like the collapsible leather tepees of the western natives, who were constantly moving to follow the buffalo herds. These were more permanent, rectangular houses with arched roofs. The frames were made of poles lashed together with vines. The covering was bark or woven matting. Not overwarm houses for the Massachusetts climate, but they served temporarily.

In spite of the care with which the Puritan migration was managed, a care which provided even clothing, the influx of settlers outran supplies. Within a year 2,000 people arrived and some went on pretty short rations. They were never in as bad shape as the settlers at Plymouth had been, but were it not for the clam and some stuff bought from the Indians, many would have starved.

MARYLAND

OF ALL THE COLONIES, excepting possibly William Penn's nearly fifty years later, Lord Baltimore's was the most intelligently conceived and the best prepared. The Maryland Indians were a poor lot. They lived largely on fish, and every time they accumulated a few skins and arrowheads, their big northern neighbors, the Susquehannocks, ambled down the shore and took everything away from them. When the settlers found them, they had already decided to move west. Governor Leonard Calvert palavered with the chiefs while his settlers were still on their two ships in the Potomac. As a result, an arrangement was made by which the colony shared an Indian village, where St. Mary's was later built, and had no hardships whatever. They were so comfortable with the Indians that Thomas Cornwalys built a water mill before he built himself a house.

NEW SWEDEN

IT WAS ON the lower Delaware and it was a beachhead and little more, but it left its mark on the country. Peter Minuit, a Dutchman who had been the first governor of New Netherland and who made the famous "purchase" of Manhattan Island, brought in a hundred Swedes and Finns on two ships in 1638. He "bought" both sides of the Delaware, from sea to sea, from the Indians for a couple of rounds of drinks and a handful of junk jewelry. The Swedes built Fort Christina, where Wilmington is now, and began to set up the kind of cabins they were used to in their own country. These could be thrown up very quickly. They were built of rough logs, with the bark still on. Both ends of each log were deeply notched on both sides and the logs were stacked, side walls and end walls alternately, with the notches resting on each other and the ends of the logs protruding both ways at the corners of the house. The rather narrow cracks left between the logs were "chinked" with chips and a mixture of clay and moss. No vertical posts were needed except at the door and the windows, if there were any windows. A stone fireplace was built at one end with a stone chimney, or sometimes one of logs and clay.

A man with only an ax for tools, and with no hardware, could build such a cabin complete. It could be covered with a thatch or bark roof on lashed poles. This was the best possible pioneer house. Its material stood in the front yard and needed to be removed anyway; but it was more than sixty years later that the German settlers in Pennsylvania, having seen these cabins on the way in, began to copy them and passed them on to the Scotch-Irish frontiersmen who made them their own.

The Swedish colony had no support from home and Peter Stuyvesant was able to march in and take it over without firing a shot. The Swedes gradually merged with the English who settled in around them. In two generations the children were speaking English and many of the family names were Anglicized. John Morton, who cast the deciding vote for the Declaration of Independence, was descended from a Swedish settler named Mortenson.

Having spotted the first immigrants about the continent, in the following pages we will look at their way of life as they dug in, as the settlements became towns, and the wilderness, farms. There are good histories which deal with wars, taxes, and government; here the concern will be with people, their food, clothes, houses, their tools and furniture, their amusements, and some of their troubles.

Swedish log cabin along the Delaware River.
The inset shows how the logs were notched

The Seventeenth Century

Seventeenth-century one-handled plow

Drawing lots for land

I. NEW ENGLAND

ONCE TEMPORARY SHELTERS had been set up and the "wolves who sat upon their tayles and grinned at us" had been driven back a little into the woods, the next order of business was to give land to each settler. At Plymouth they tried holding all the land in common, but it didn't work. At Salem and Boston and other later towns, a space was set aside for the church and a large area as a common pasture; what remained was divided up as building sites. The choice locations went to the governor, the ministers, and the other elite in strict order of precedence, the rest being distributed by lot among the common folk.

In addition to a town plot, each family was given outlying land for farming when and as they could clear it. This is what most of them had come for. As the land was taken up, new towns were started and the process of division was repeated.

It was thus that Connecticut was founded. For example, a whole congregation, headed by its preacher, would trek off into the wilderness and set up a town.

House Building

Once a settler had his own lot, the next step was to put a livable house on it. In nearly every case that meant he had to put the house together himself with what help he could muster. In addition, he had to cut the trees and shape the lumber before construction could begin.

Except that nobody used a saw on standing timber, trees were felled much as they still are, but the squaring of timbers with a broadax is a craft few now practice, or know how to do. An oak log of

Squaring timber with a broadax

The adz and its use in dressing a large timber

the required length was placed across two other logs and braced so that it couldn't roll. The bracing could be done by spiking one end of a stick into the upper side of the main log and spiking the other end into one of the supporting logs.

The hewer, standing with the log on his left, made a series of back-cuts, across the grain, all the way down the side nearer him. The chips between the cuts were then split out and a new set of cuts was made until that face of the timber was down far enough to form one side of the largest square that could be cut from the log. The log was turned and the operation was repeated on the other three sides. Squaring a big timber took a couple of hours when an expert did the job.

A broadax had a short handle and a wide, almost straight blade. It was kept very sharp. The last layer of chips on each face was hewn away with the edge, instead of being just roughly split off. This gave a fair finish, but the marks of the back-cuts and of the hewing were still visible. If the timber was to be used where it could be seen, say in a ceiling, its surface was carefully finished with an adz. This was an ax shaped like a hoe. On a large timber the adz-man stood on the surface he was smoothing and cut toward his own toes; a small timber he straddled. Either way required care; a slip was easy to make and, but for its size, a man might shave with a properly sharpened adz. A plane could do a slicker job than an adz but not too much slicker.

With a sufficient supply of squared timbers laid aside, the settler had next to plan his house and provide a foundation for it. None of the first cottages has survived, but it is doubtful that many of them had more than one room. The method of building and the general plan followed what the settlers were used to seeing in England, with one notable exception: these houses had cellars. A cellar made a warmer house, but that wasn't the primary reason for having one. It was for frost-free storage. The cellar had a dirt floor but its walls were stone, carried just a little above the ground surface, as a foundation for the house. Brick was made in Massachusetts, but stone lay everywhere free for the taking. Cement was unknown and lime for mortar was scarcer than hen's teeth, so the stones were laid with mud. While he was in stonework the builder began the big chimney. The outside measurement of a one-room house would be about twenty-eight by twenty-two feet; of this, a corner space ten feet by twelve would be devoted to the chimney.

The next job was to fit a wooden sill on top of the stone foundation. The sill was made of squared timbers, good heavy ones, lapped over at the corners, with square-cornered holes, or mortises, cut through them wherever a post was to stand. A one-room house needed eight posts: three across the front wall, three across the back, and two at the front corners of the chimney. At the foot of each post, enough wood was cut away to leave a tenon which would fit into its proper mortise in the sill. Individual mortises and tenons were made to fit together and were numbered with a Roman numeral scribed on the wood, so they could be properly matched. When they were put together a hole would be bored straight through the sill and the tenon, and a wooden pin called a treenail (pronounced "trunnel") was driven into the hole. Mortises were cut through the upper end of each post for the upper beams but the post was not put

A mortise-and-tenon joint with its treenail

into place when it was finished. It and its brothers were laid aside until all the timbers for the house had been shaped, then, lying on the ground with the toes of the posts near their mortises, the front and back walls were assembled into "broadsides." The front and rear girts, as the upper beams were called, were fitted into the posts and pinned. The end girts and the chimney girts and plenty of treenails were put where they could be grabbed in a hurry. Then it was time to have a "raisin' " party.

Lashings of food and drink were assembled and the neighbors were invited over. The men were divided into groups. One bunch raised the front wall, another the back one. The broadsides were lifted by hand as far as the men could reach, then pushed the rest of the way up with long poles, called pikes from their resemblance to the weapon of that name. Pikes are still used to raise utility poles and the procedure is similar.

As the posts reached a vertical position, the tenons on their butts were guided into the mortises prepared for them in the sill, and a small crew, standing in the cellar, used pikes to keep the frames from going over too far. Then, while both walls were steadied, two other groups raised the end girts, slipped the tenons into their mortises, and drove home the treenails that would hold

them there. It took quite a gang of men to accomplish the thing and it is easier to read about than to do.

Once the basic frame was erected, the family could go ahead and finish the house without further help except perhaps for getting the "summer" in place. The summer was a jumbo-size beam, as large as ten inches by fourteen, that ran the long way across the ceiling. It was mortised into the end girt and the chimney girt in a tricky way, so that its own weight held it in place, with no pin needed. Square recesses were spaced along both of the upper edges of the summer and the sidewall girts, to receive the ends of the joists to which the attic floor was nailed. This floor was also the ceiling of the downstairs room; there was no applied ceiling of any kind. The joists for the first floor were simply logs with their bark still on; nobody could see them, they were in the cellar.

Planking for floors and for lining the walls inside had to be sawn. There were no sawmills at first so the work was done with a long pit saw, or a sash saw, set in a frame. A piece of squared timber was placed on supports laid across a deep pit. The sawyer, who guided the saw along a chalk line, stood on the timber above ground. His assistant, the pitman, worked below in a shower of

31

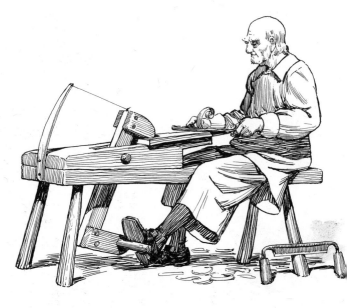

A saw-pit with a sash saw in use.
In the foreground is an ordinary pit saw

sawdust and furnished the pull for the downward, cutting stroke.

Set about two feet apart between the posts to fill out the wall frame, and lighter than the main timbers, the studs were usually sawn. So were the corner braces that stiffened the house against the wind, and so were the roof rafters, unless they were left as poles in the rough.

The roofs were steep. There was no ridgepole but the rafters were connected by several long timbers on each slope. These were known as purlins. Light poles were fastened across the upper surface of the rafters and bundles of rushes, or straw, were lashed to them in overlapping rows to thatch the roof. This didn't leak except in wet weather and it would last as long as thirty years if it didn't catch fire.

About mid-century, roofs began to be sheathed with boards and surfaced with shingles. The shingles were riven with a froe like clapboards, except that they were split flat across the full width of a log. They were from a foot and a half to three feet long. At first shingles were used in the rough state, just as split, but they did their job better if they were shaved flat and tapered with a drawknife. For this job, an ingenious, foot-operated clamp called a shingle horse was used.

The spaces between the wall studs were filled

The construction of a New England seventeenth-century house. Studs are omitted from the front wall for clarity

32

with nogging as insulation, the outside of the wall being covered with unpainted clapboards and the inside with pine sheathing boards, some of them two feet wide. The nogging at first was made of rolls of straw-bonded clay, later bricks were used and some houses may have been built with the brick nogging exposed, as was often done in England. Bricks were made at Salem very early.

One-room houses had their chimneys in one corner. Between the side of the chimney and the front wall a small inside vestibule was built. It was called a porch but it was completely enclosed. Into it the front door opened and, against the chimney side of it, a narrow stair or a ladder of pegs led to the boys' sleeping quarters in the attic.

Windows were made small to conserve heat. The first ones were "glazed" with oiled paper. When glass was imported it came in small pieces and was very expensive; both things helped to keep window-sizes small. They had diamond-shaped panes set in strips of lead and about one in three of them was hinged so that it could be opened. Most of the sash were about a foot wide and two feet high. They were placed high up in the wall, the sill about four feet from the floor. A few people made larger windows by setting two or three sash side by side. Practically all American windows before 1700 were of leaded glass but only a few of them survived the Revolution, when their lead was commandeered for bullets.

When a house was to have two rooms, or when more space had to be added, the second room was built to the left of the porch. Such a room seems to have been called the parlor, and the original room was then designated as the hall or the keeping-room. Even with two rooms, the keeping-room was used for cooking, eating, and sleeping. A two-story house of this type usually had its second floor projected a foot or so on the front wall, or on both ends, or on all three, but almost never on the back.

A second story had to have posts like the first. When it projected, its posts were extended downward, below the level of the first floor girts, and the exposed ends were carved into a square acorn shape. Some of the kinds of houses that were built are shown in the village illustration a little further on in the section about towns. In the second half of the century, when Indians became troublesome, "garrison houses" were built along the outer fringes of the settled area. These had solid walls of hewn timbers laid one on top of another, but they weren't strictly log cabins, because the timbers were squared and didn't project at the corners. These garrison houses were forts, of course. Many of them had solid "Indian shutters" on the insides of the windows.

As families grew, and in spite of an appalling death rate they did grow, a "linter" (lean-to) was built against the back wall to provide space for a kitchen, a pantry, and a bedroom, with a low attic over them. The resulting shape came to be known as a "saltbox" house and toward the end of the seventeenth century new houses were intentionally built that shape.

The saltbox house had three fireplaces all using the same chimney stack but there was no heat in the downstairs bedroom or in the pantry. It was found that the best place for a chimney in this cold climate was in the center of the house; then any warmth that came from it was used. Wood was burned in the fireplaces, sometimes logs so big that they had to be dragged in through the back door by a horse. Even so the houses were not very warm. Men have recorded the ink freezing on their pens as they wrote sitting close to the fire!

Any necessary outbuilding, such as a woodshed, a privy, or a barn, was built at first of wattle-and-daub on a rough pole frame. Later, barns were built with hewn-timber frames like the houses; in fact, barns continued to be built that way long after a lighter and less laborious construction was used for dwellings.

Wells

It's unlikely that each house had its own well just at first, but one was dug as soon as the owner could get around to it. When he did, it was merely a round hole in the ground, lined with stones laid "dry," without mortar that is. The stone wall was

A well sweep

carried about three feet above the surface to keep children and animals from falling in. The country was covered with trees, which kept the water table near the surface, so a well didn't have to be very deep. Occasionally a well was dug in a cellar.

To get water from the well, a bucket on a rope was dropped in and then hauled out hand-over-hand when it had filled. That was hard work. It had to be done in an awkward position, leaning over the coping, and water is heavy. The sweep, a long pole lying in the crotch of an upright forked post, made the job easier. The longer end of the pole extended over the well and had another pole hanging from its tip; to the lower end of this the "old oaken bucket" was attached. The short end of the sweep pole had a wooden cradle at its extremity that held enough stones to balance the weight of a bucket of water. The work had to be done in getting the empty bucket *down* the well, but it was a lot easier work than hauling the full bucket up; it could be done by a child, and was. There are well sweeps still in use in America.

Furniture

For furniture inside his house the settler had what little he had brought with him, what he could afford to have a "joyner" make for him, and what he could make himself. The amount of furni-

ture said to have "come over on the *Mayflower*" is a standing and rather tired joke. Actually there is just one piece in existence that certainly came in the first consignment, a wicker cradle. But other ships came and they brought not only some back-breaking wainscot chairs but also useful chests and almost equally useful crates. A table exists which has lettered on its underside the name and address of the immigrant to whom it was consigned as part of a crate.

Wainscot chairs were direct descendants of medieval thrones and were very little different from them, being made for dignity but not for comfort. The chair against the wall in the keeping-room is a wainscot chair. A few pages further on, in the drawing of the Puritan family at dinner, the goodman sits in another kind of chair that was just as uncomfortable, but somewhat lighter. It has been called a Carver chair, from the Pilgrim governor who owned one. The leading Elder of Plymouth had a chair quite like it, but with many more spindles, and his name, Brewster, has been given to it. They are really two versions of the same thing.

Most homemade furniture was put together from lumber cut and sawn on the place. It was heavy and simple. There couldn't be much of it, because there wasn't room in the house. Often there were no chairs, or at best but one, for the

The "keeping-room" of an early New England house

man of the family. Stools and long benches, called forms, were common, and so was another kind of bench called a settle. It usually was so narrow that it was barely possible to sit on it, but it had a very high, solid back that gave protection from drafts on bitter winter nights.

The earliest tables were nearly all made of oak, long and narrow, to seat as many people as possible in a minimum of space. The tops were as thick as two inches and were supported on a trestle frame which had only two legs. The Puritan family on page 39 is about to eat from one of these tables. Gate-leg and other folding tables were also made after a few years, always with that idea of saving floor space. There was even a bench with a movable back that converted into a table. For the same reason some beds came to be hinged near the head so that they could be raised out of the way in the daytime; and when ladder-back chairs became plentiful, they were hung up on pegs when they weren't in use.

These houses had no closets, little cupboards now and then for tobacco and liquor and ink, but no real closets. Extra clothes were hung from a row of pegs set in a board on the wall, or from pegs driven into holes in the wall itself. Linen and blankets were stored in chests that at first had no drawers; they were merely boxes with hinged lids. Drawers were added later and space could then be saved by stacking one chest on top of another. Even quite poor people were likely to own large quantities of linen—and it really *was* linen, not cotton; they had to have enough to last a month or even three months, from one Gargantuan wash-day to the next.

In the first one-room houses, the owner and his wife slept in a "jack bed" built into one corner. This kind didn't fold; its head and one side were supported by the walls and it needed only one post, at its outer corner. Like most seventeenth- and eighteenth-century beds, the jack bed was high from the floor and quite short, because nobody slept lying flat; he reclined in a half-sitting position on several big goose-feather pillows. An extremely low trundle bed, for a child, was kept under the big bed and pulled out at night. The cradle for the baby (there was always a baby) was set near the fire.

The custom of "bundling" that prevailed at this time seems to have been nothing more than

A jack bed and a trundle bed

a practical way to provide warmth and chaperoned privacy for a courting couple under difficult conditions. The family occupied the hearth; so the young people were tucked up in the jack bed, to do their whispering in full view of parental eyes.

No matter how many blankets are put on, the unaided human body has a bad time trying to warm up a really cold bed. The situation could be helped a lot by prewarming a bed with a warming pan. Such a pan was made of brass or copper and had a pierced lid and a long wooden handle. A few hot embers from the fire were put into the pan and it was passed between the sheets. It had to be kept moving or it would scorch them.

Food

Food was available to the settlers for the getting, but not without effort and not of much variety. Indian corn was the mainstay of diet throughout the seventeenth century. This was true of the whole country, not only of the North. Most families ate it 365 days a year, and for long periods in the early days the fare was corn and little else. The methods of grinding it and the recipes for cooking it, as well as its cultivation, were all learned from the Indians. As time passed the settlers made improvements in all of these things. They cleared fields and plowed; they set up mills; and they learned to mix things like rye flour (wheat didn't do well in New England at first), milk, and eggs with their corn meal. Some of their formulas are still followed and eaten with relish.

Warming pan

A samp mortar

Before they ground it in a stone or wooden mortar the Indians cooked their corn, and the settlers started out using the same system. Not all corn was ground to fine meal. Some was merely hulled and eaten whole as hominy; some was broken into coarse grains and boiled as a porridge called samp. Samp was pounded in a mortar hollowed out of the upper end of a three-foot post. The pestle was a billet tied to the top of a bent-over sapling. The sapling lifted the pestle, and all the housewife had to do was pound it down. This she did for hours at a time. It was said that mariners in fog knew they were getting into shallow water when they could hear the thump of the samp mortars.

In time some of the mortars were replaced by samp mills, or querns. A quern consisted of two flat, circular, grinding stones set one upon the other. The lower one was fixed; the upper had a funnel-shaped hole through its center and a smaller hole near its edge for the end of the stick that made a handle for rotating it. The grain was poured into the funnel; the ground meal worked out from between the stones around the outside. The quern is older than history. A windmill, which frightened the Indians, was built in Massachusetts in 1631, almost before there was any grain to grind, and a water mill was added shortly, but most people went on grinding at home for many years.

Corn was also eaten green, as it is now. Usually it was roasted in embers, in its own husk. We still speak of "roasting ears," though few are now roasted. Sometimes green corn was cut off the cob and boiled as what the Indians called *sukquttahash;* both the word and the dish have been amended.

Corn was of such importance that it was itself the standard of value and was used as money. The settlers raised good crops on the virgin soil; eighty-six bushels from one bushel of seed has been recorded. They were able to trade their surplus to the Indians for game and pelts. Corn was ordinarily stored in attics and, after the harvest, there wasn't much room up there for the youngsters to sleep. The corn had to be shelled off the cob before it could be ground. That was a job done in front of the fire on winter evenings by the small fry, who scraped the kernels off on the edge of a shovel, or against the long handle of a pan, laid across a wooden bucket. Corncobs were saved for kindling, and for smoking meat.

Of the other native American vegetables, the pumpkin was perhaps the most useful. It could be dried and kept for winter; in fact it would keep fresh if it was put in a dry, cool place and kept from freezing, but that was difficult. A pumpkin could be roasted whole, or mashed up and mixed with corn meal to make "punkin bread."

English vegetables and fruits were planted. Grass seed for pastures had to be imported, as no good native grass was found at first. With the seed came the seeds of English weeds which moved right in and have now taken such hold that we think of them as natives. The broad-leaved plantain is one of the many; the Indians named it "the

Grinding corn meal with a quern

white man's foot," because it seemed to spring up wherever he trod.

Meat at first was largely game. Though the settlers hunted, they depended heavily on barter with the Indians to get meat, especially as the larger game moved further from the towns. Fishing, clamming, and lobstering were carried on by the settlers but in this field too trade filled out supplies. The preservation of meat was always a difficulty; most of it had to be salted, or smoked, or pickled. The demand for pepper and other spices was largely due to their usefulness in concealing the taste of overripe meat.

Cooking

Some special cooking projects that were large operations, like rendering lard and making apple butter, were done outdoors, but all day-to-day cookery was done in the fireplace. The masonry itself was planned for wood-fire cooking as well as for warmth. All of the fireplaces were large; those in New England were usually four or five feet high; curiously it is in the South that cooking fireplaces high enough for a man to walk into are found. A heavy hewn timber, called the "mantel tree," was used as a lintel to support the stonework above the fireplace opening. The wood might be scorched occasionally, but it was far enough in front of the rising column of heat to be safe from fire.

On the inside of the chimney, above the mantel tree, two ledges were made. On these rested the ends of a lug pole from which pots were suspended to cook. Green wood was used for the lug pole, so it would resist heat, but it had to be renewed frequently because it dried out and charred and was weakened. Sometimes people forgot to put in a new pole soon enough and the dinner fell into the fire. There are records of tragic scaldings from this accident. When iron became easier to get, it was used instead of wood for lug poles, and later fireplaces had gudgeons built into them for hanging a swinging crane.

Beside the fireplace and built as part of it was the oven. It was made like a small, secondary fireplace with a flue of its own leading into the main chimney. Sometimes the door of the oven faced the room, but most of them were built with the opening facing the hearth. The later ones (they

Stone oven.
On the hearth is a bake kettle and a bean pot

were used into the nineteenth century) all had hinged iron doors, but in primitive times they were closed with wood and clay. The oven flue, too, had to be closed in some way.

Baking was done once or twice a week in most houses. On baking days a roaring fire of "oven wood," which was maple sticks, was maintained in the oven until its walls were deeply hot. While the oven was heating the dough was mixed and set to rise on the hearth. After supper the embers were scraped out of the oven, its flue was closed, and some leaves were spread on its floor. The loaves were slid in on a flat wooden shovel called a peel or slice, and twitched off onto the leaves. The peel had a little meal sprinkled on it so the dough wouldn't stick to it. Then the front openings were sealed as tightly as possible. Once the oven was closed, the good wife could get a night's sleep and take out her bread in the morning, brown, fragrant, and crusty. People who have eaten bread baked that way will tell you that no other compares with it and certainly it bore little relation to the "wet cotton" that passes for bread today.

Not all baking was done in the big oven. There was also an iron "bake kettle" that looked like a stewpot on legs and that had an iron lid. This is said to have done an excellent baking job when it was banked with embers in the fireplace and had more embers piled on its lid. It was used chiefly for biscuits, shortbread, and pone. The name "Dutch oven" has confusingly been given to this pot, to the big stone oven, and to the eighteenth-century sheet metal "roasting kitchen."

Roasting meat on a spit

Pot hooks and a trammel

Meat wasn't ever baked, except in pies, and even then it was mostly precooked. It was a great time for stews or "spoon meat," and much of the meat was minced and cooked in a pot. By bringing a big stew to a boil every day it could be kept presentable for some time without refrigeration. Of course some fresh meat was broiled and some was fried and a lot of it was roasted.

The standard roaster was a spit, three feet long or more, that was thrust clear through the meat. It had a crank at one end for turning it and a couple of prongs, made near the same end, that stuck into the meat and forced it to turn with the spit. The ends of the rod were supported, sometimes, on hooks that were part of the andirons. A shallow pan on the hearth caught the drippings with which the roast was basted. Constant turning cooked the meat evenly and it was a child's dull chore to turn the spit. Lacking an iron spit, and many did lack one, the meat could be suspended on a double string in front of the fire and given a spin now and then. Never pity your ancestors for the quality of their cookery. Once they had conquered the supply problem, they ate the best there ever was.

The height of a stewpot above the fire had to be adjusted according to the heat of the fire and the rapidity with which it was desired to boil the pot. This was done from the earliest days with pothooks of various lengths. A pothook was a light iron rod with hooked ends turned away from each other so that it looked like the letter S. Before the seventeenth century was out, an adjustable pothook called a trammel had been introduced. The best way to describe a trammel is to draw it. The teeth on the edge of the lower rod hung on swinging stirrups attached to the upper rod, giving a wide choice of lengths.

Utensils for cooking necessarily had long handles. Pots and pans came in great variety. Before fireplace cooking was abandoned devices had been made to parallel every modern kitchen utensil, and there were some which have no modern counterpart. A lot of the old things still exist, partly because they were metal, and partly because of the way many of them were discarded. When cookstoves came into use, fireplaces had to be closed up to accommodate them. The long-handled pans with legs on them were useless with a stove, so, in one house after another, they were tossed into the fireplace and walled up, as the easiest way of getting rid of them. Some of them are still there.

Though some dippers and strainers were brass, everything else used near the fire was iron. In addition to having long handles, skillets had quite long legs, so they would sit up above the embers. Broilers had legs, too. Refinements like toasters and plate warmers came later; the early settlers did their toasting on long forks. They did have iron stands called trivets on which a pot of food could be set to keep warm near the fire.

Eating and Drinking

The customs connected with eating and drinking change with the years, and those of the seventeenth century seem odd to us now. Today we think a man is far gone in sin when he drinks be-

strainer

bake kettle

trivet

sauce-pan

gridiron (broiler)

toasting fork

spider (frying pan)

Iron cooking utensils

Puritans at dinner

fore breakfast; in the 1600's everybody had a "morning draft" of beer or ale, even children. In time the New Englanders changed to hard cider, but the custom persisted. John Hancock, who signed the Declaration of Independence with such a flourish, thought of himself as an abstemious man, yet he had a pint of hard cider every morning before breakfast! In the hard, early days of Boston no beer was available; John Winthrop's family had to resort to water and he notes with surprise in his diary that it seemed to agree with them.

When mealtime came in a New England household, the goodman and his older boys sat down to the table with their hats on. The custom of wearing hats indoors, even at church, was usual everywhere in the seventeenth century; it lasted until after men began to wear wigs. If there was a serving wench, or a daughter old enough to serve, the wife sat down too, not at the far end of the table but next to her husband. The younger children stood at the table and, in absolute silence, ate what was given to them. In some houses children ate, standing, at a separate table. They were forbidden to take salt except with a clean knife, or to throw bones on the floor.

Very simple folk sometimes put the cooking pot on the table and the whole family ate directly from it; but most people ladled the food onto wooden trenchers and ate from them, each

trencher being shared by two diners. A trencher was a wooden slab with a shallow depression hollowed into one side of it. Even when the century was half gone a deacon, who owned a lathe, was criticized for putting on airs when he turned out a separate trencher for each of his children. His trenchers were probably round; most of them weren't made on lathes, so they were rectangular. A few families owned big, pewter chargers on which they brought food to the table.

Clean linen napkins were needed for every meal, because people ate with their fingers. It can't be said that forks for eating didn't exist; Governor Winthrop owned just one, a "double dagger," two-tined and in a leather case. He probably used it about as often as you would use a

A pewter charger and a wooden trencher

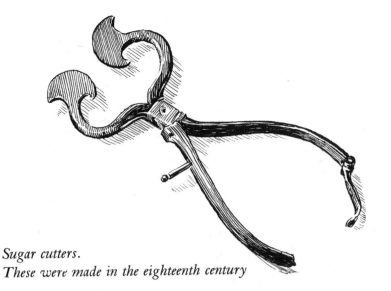

Sugar cutters.
These were made in the eighteenth century

wooden trencher. If the nature of the food was such that fingers couldn't handle it, it was eaten with a spoon. If meat needed to be cut, you took your own knife out of its sheath, and cut it. Spoons were made of wood, of horn, and of pewter. Silver spoons were known in England, though few were used; there were almost none on this side of the water until after 1650. Pewter is easily melted, so, when spoons broke or wore out, they could be re-cast in a gun-metal mold.

Honey was used on New England tables; but the Indians always insisted there were no bees in America until the white men came. They called bees "English flies." The settlers learned from the Indians to make sugar by boiling down maple sap. In time they came to import molasses, but not much cane sugar was seen for many years. When it did appear, it came in solid, beehive-shaped

loaves. These had to be broken apart and the chunks were cut into usable size with curious shears whose blades didn't quite come together. Anyone who owns a pair of these will find they are unbeatable for cutting up hard candy.

Salt was highly valued. Most of it had to be imported from Spain and the Cape Verde Islands. Attempts to make it from sea water didn't have much success at first. There were no individual salt cellars on seventeenth-century tables. Salt was put into a single large saler in the middle of the table, just as it had been in medieval days, and social rank was still evidenced by one's position at the table, above or below the salt. Bread was not sliced but broken, and no butter was spread on it in New England, though it would be hard to believe it wasn't sopped in the gravy.

Along with the trenchers and spoons, there were wooden noggins and tankards for milk if the family owned a cow, and for beer whether there was a cow or not. There were pewter mugs for drinking, and some made of boiled leather, called "black jacks," black for their color, jack from their material. Boiled leather was generally known as jacked leather; jack boots got their name the same way. Black jacks were sewn together with waxed linen thread and rimmed with pewter, copper, or silver. Seeing them in use in England once led a Frenchman to report at home that the English drank out of their boots!

When a meal ended, a basket called a voider was passed around the table and everything that had been used, including the napkins, was put into it to be taken away and washed. Then father

A tankard, a "black jack," and a noggin, with a clay pipe and smoking tongs

Fire scoop

*Tinderbox and flint-and-steel in use.
The inset is an enlargement of the steel*

and mother and the older children and the serving maid (some families had them; they came cheap) would stuff tobacco into their clay pipes and light up with a hot ember lifted from the fire with tongs. Small tongs called smoking tongs came to be made for this special purpose.

Heat and Light

There were no matches to strike and it was hard to get a fire started, so an effort was made to keep one going all the time, winter and summer. At night the embers were banked with ashes to slow down burning and keep at least a few sparks until morning. Sometimes this failed and no amount of puffing and fanning would start the blaze again. Then a child would be sent to a neighbor's with a fire scoop, to borrow a few hot coals. If there was no neighbor, it was necessary to start a new fire by striking sparks from flint and steel into tinder. Tinder was anything that would ignite easily; the commonest was charred shreds of linen. It was kept, with the flint and steel, in a metal tinderbox that usually had a socket on its top for a candle, used to hold the flame once the tinder had caught. To light the tinder, the chunk of flint was held in the left hand, over the open tinderbox, and was struck a glancing blow with the steel, so that sparks were thrown downward. The appearance of the slightest glow on the rags was a signal to commence a blowing operation that might succeed in nursing the spark into a small flame. Charles Dickens, who had made a fire that way, said that with luck it could be done in half an

hour. That would be a long half-hour on a January morning, with the fire out.

Once flame had been kindled, it was quickly transferred to the tinderbox candle, or to a sliver of pitch pine, and applied to a handful of shavings or splinters to start the fire. Starting a fire with paper would have been unthinkable; paper was far too valuable.

Up to the eighteenth century no improvement had been made in artificial lighting for three thousand years or more. The lighting used at Plymouth and Boston was not more primitive than what was being used then in London and Paris; in fact, the settlers were better off, for they had unlimited wood for bright fires and they had the American pitch pine that would blaze brightly, if somewhat smokily, from its own resin. A torch of this "light wood" or "candle wood" could be lit and stuck between two flagstones on the hearth and most of the smoke would go up the chimney. This means of lighting was generally called a "candle set."

Aside from the pine torches, all light was obtained by burning fat or wax in some way. The commonest way was the rushlight, which was made by soaking the pith of a dried rush in grease. When it was saturated it was pinched in the jaws of a special holder and its projecting end was lighted. It not only smoked, it stank. It needed constant attention, because as soon as it burned back to the jaws of the holder it went out. The holders were made in many forms: with hooks to hang on the edge of a shelf; with spikes to be driven into a beam; with bases to sit on a table; and with

A rushlight, a tall candleholder, and a portable candlestick

light of these things, though it's hard to see how they did it.

There were few candles at first because of the lack of material to make them. When the sheep population increased enough to provide tallow, candles became more plentiful, but they were sparingly used. It was found that really good candles could be made from the wax of bayberries. These were the grayish-white fruit of a low bush which grew, and still grows, everywhere along the Atlantic coast. The sage-green candles were of such quality that in time they were exported and were welcomed in Europe, not only because they gave a good clean light, but also because they smelled good when they were extinguished. Anything which gave light and smelled good, too, was a novelty; people liked to scent a room by extinguishing the candles for a few minutes before company was expected.

Most candles, especially at first, were made by dipping. Depending on the size of the wax pot, six or eight wick strings were hung a couple of inches apart on sticks called candle rods. The wicks were laid across the stick at their middles and the

legs to stand on the floor. Most of them were iron and sometimes the weighted end, which kept the jaws closed, had a candle socket on it.

Grease was also burned in the so-called "betty lamps," as it had been before Athens was founded. The name seems to come from the Early English word *bettyngs,* meaning oil or fat. Basically this kind of lamp was a shallow grease-filled metal dish, with a lip in which lay a linen wick burning just beyond the lip. It was better than the rush-light because the wick absorbed new grease as it burned and so needed less care. A betty lamp ordinarily had a handle that curved inward over the grease dish and had attached to its end a chain terminating in a combination spike and hook for hanging the lamp. On the same chain was hung a sharp pick about two inches long, for pulling the wick out to make it burn brighter. Any kind of grease was burned; much use was made of bear fat, deer fat, fish oil, and even passenger pigeon fat; and our forebears complained of the smell of all of them. When domestic animals became plentiful, their fat was used; but it didn't smell any better. People worked and even read by the

*An adjustable
hanging candleholder*

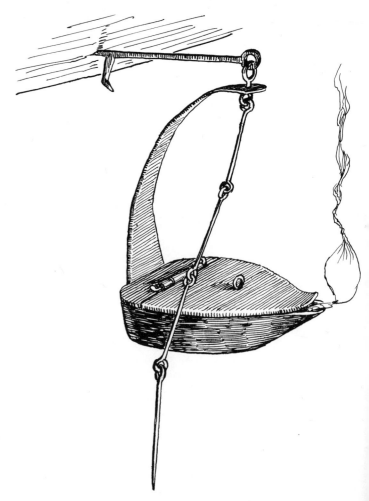

A "betty lamp" for burning grease

two parts were twisted together below it; this gave a desirably thicker wick and produced the bottom loop that was characteristic of all Colonial candles. The wax was melted and the wicks were repeatedly dipped in the pot a rodful at a time. After each dipping they were set aside to cool, the ends of the rods resting on parallel poles set up for the purpose. Experience was needed to keep the pot at the right temperature; if it was too cool the candle came out lumpy; if it was too hot it would melt off the wax already deposited. On a cool day, a good dipper could make a couple of hundred candles.

After life became settled enough for artisans to set up shop, it was possible to buy metal candle molds that made candle-making much simpler; but they didn't eliminate the dipping process. These molds were tapered tubes made of sheet iron (called tin) or, more rarely, of pewter. They were made in connected groups of from two to two dozen. In any group the upper ends of the molds, which would make the bottoms of the finished candles, all opened into a shallow pan into which wax was poured. The bottoms of the tubes were closed except for a hole in each just big enough for a wick. Wicks were threaded through the holes and were looped over small sticks laid across the pan at the top of the mold. The whole mold was filled with hot wax and set aside to cool. In cooling the wax shrank enough for the finished candles to be pulled out.

Candle-molding and a finished molded candle

After a while it became customary for traveling candle-makers or chandlers to bring their own large molds to a house and make up the family's accumulated stock of tallow and wax into candles. They were seldom given any actual money for the job; they took "country pay" in the form of extra wax, or almost any other product of the household that both parties could agree upon. Benjamin Franklin's father was a candle-maker, "a tallow and wax chandeler."

Home Crafts

For a long time Northerners who needed any article had to make it for themselves. It was possible to import things from England if you had money or credit, but few had either. In the South the export of tobacco established credit in England and the planters did import much of what they needed; but the North had no great export at first, and by the time trade got going the people had acquired the habit of supplying their own needs.

All grease was saved; it was not only valuable for lighting, it was also the basis of soap. Wood ashes were saved, too; they supplied soap's other ingredient, lye. The ashes were thrown into a barrel between layers of straw, a little water was poured in now and then, and lye dripped out of a

Candle-dipping and its product

Boiling soap

seep hole at the bottom of the barrel. The straw kept the coarser part of the ashes from clogging the hole. To the accompaniment of a ghastly odor, grease and lye were boiled together in big iron kettles, out in the open air. The mess was con-

stantly stirred and it cooked into a harsh soft soap. For some reason the operation wasn't always successful, and it was hence a courtesy to wish a neighbor luck with her soap. To promote the luck the soap was always stirred in one direction only. Soft soap could be hardened by the addition of salt, but not much salt was wasted that way.

Iron was sparingly used even in Europe during the seventeenth century. In the Colonies, though early attempts were made to start iron works, not much of it was to be had at any price. What there was was used for cooking pots, and tools, where no other material could be substituted.

The settlers, and their descendants for years, had to find ways of making wood do the work of iron. Door hinges and latches were made of tough wood. We still make wooden barrels, but those intended for liquids have iron hoops. Colonial barrel hoops were made of hickory and ash. Buckets were made of wooden staves and looked like small tubs. Two staves on opposite sides were left longer than the rest and were pierced near their tops to serve as handles. Bails were put on iron cooking pots, but a bucket of water was carried by a stick put through the holes in the long staves or by a short rope tied from hole to hole. Piggins, which were smaller than buckets, were made the same way, except that they had only one long stave,

Door latch of wood

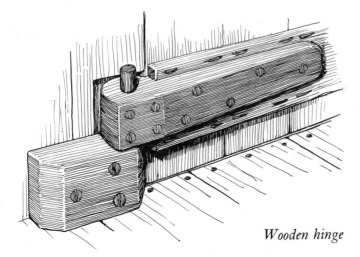

Wooden hinge

44

sometimes pierced but more often shaped into a handle to be grasped.

All of these things, barrels, pails, and piggins, were made by professional coopers, who were possibly the first artisans to ply a trade in America. Even so, there weren't many coopers and in most houses homemade substitutes for their work had to be made by laboriously hollowing out logs. Even big barrels for the storage of salted meat were excavated from tree trunks three feet across. The Indians used fire to help in clearing out the insides of their log boats and no doubt the colonists copied the method. It involved constant fanning or blowing.

Since much carrying of water was done daily, every family whittled out nicely fitting human neck yokes that reduced the arm strain of carrying two buckets at once. In the illustration of the Puritan huts on page 24 there is a man using a neck yoke. The heavy yoke that coupled a span of oxen and by which they pulled a cart was made entirely of wood; so probably was the cart they pulled. Two centuries later Western pioneers built the Red River cart without an ounce of iron in it anywhere, because they had no iron to put in it. There is very early mention of a wheelwright being brought to New England but nothing is known of his product, except what can be guessed from English oxcarts of the time. It's even possible that he didn't build vehicles at all but made spinning wheels. The term "wheelwright" covered both crafts.

The list of Colonial wooden articles is long; even spades were carved, handle and blade together, from a single wooden billet, though it's safe

A hollow-log barrel

to say that such a one was never used in preference to an iron spade. The wooden hayfork may have had some advantage over a metal fork, if only in the way of lightness. There's a drawing of one of them in the section on New Netherland.

In addition to their wooden trenchers, noggins, and spoons, the settlers made bowls of the knobs, called burls, that grew on some maple trees. They learned the trick from the Indians. The natural shape of a burl is like the bottom of a bowl, so it only had to be cleaned up and hollowed out. Only! Burl grain runs crazily in all directions, so a bowl made from one didn't readily split.

Wooden spade

Cloth

The new Americans had to provide clothes for themselves. Cloth and made-up garments could be imported from England and in the South they usually were, but again the North lacked the money for that. There was also the chilling fear of importing the plague along with the clothes, which, if one happened to bring in the right flea, tucked into the seam of a doublet, would have been entirely possible. On the other hand, it would

A barrel, a piggin, a churn, and a bucket

never have occurred to anyone then to refrain from wearing a garment merely because it had a few fleas in it.

Producing one's own clothes meant not merely tailoring them; it also meant weaving the cloth to be tailored, and spinning the yarn to be woven, and raising and preparing the material to be spun.

Linen was first, because flax can be sown in May and harvested at the end of June. Wool takes a full year to grow on the animal, and it takes some years to develop a flock of sheep by breeding. So flax was grown in 1640, and though it is estimated there were 3,000 sheep in New England in 1644 their wool wasn't enough to clothe the population.

Wool Production

Though linen may have been produced sooner in America, it makes better sense to deal first with the making of wool yarn. The operation was simpler; so was the wheel on which wool was spun.

Wool is the winter coat of fleece sheared from a sheep when the weather has warmed up enough for the animal to get along without it. The shearing is an expert operation that should get the complete fleece off in one piece without wounding the sheep. It is done now with power clippers. Originally it was done with hand shears that looked a lot like spring-backed grass clippers.

Many of the Massachusetts Bay settlers had been clothiers at home (a clothier then made cloth, not clothes), so they were well acquainted with wool-processing. It was first necessary to get out of the fleece all the trash that the sheep had managed to pick up, bits of pine tar, sticks, and burrs, as well as "feltings," places where the wool had become matted into hopeless knots. The fleece was then thoroughly scoured, and when this had been done it was often dyed "in the wool."

Indigo was the favorite dye; it was blue, of course. Madder was used for red, if it could be had. These two were importations. They were

Carding wool

supplemented by yellows and browns made by boiling various tree barks and roots. Hickory, walnut, oak, and sassafras were used. A few flowers and berries yielded dyes which could be "set" as permanent color, among them goldenrod, iris, and pokeberry.

Along with the dirt, scouring removed all the natural grease from the fleece, and it had to be saturated with lard oil before it would submit to carding. Carding was a job for grandmothers who weren't able to do much else and who had no teeth to be set on edge by it. Its object was to fluff the wool and mix it thoroughly and evenly, not to straighten it, as has sometimes been said. It was done with two rectangular paddles, both set thickly with wire teeth that curved back a little toward the handles.

A small bunch of wool was put between them and one paddle was pulled repeatedly across the other with the teeth opposed. To strip the carded "sliver" of wool out, the moving (upper) paddle was reversed and the two cards were rubbed gently back and forth against each other. The resulting sliver was ready to be spun into ordinary woolen yarn. If it was desired to spin worsted, in which the fibers are laid as parallel as possible, a further combing operation was needed that straightened the fibers and removed the short ones.

Wool-Spinning

Spinning is simply twisting. You'll find that you can pull fibers partly out of a wad of ordinary absorbent cotton and twist them into a short crude thread between your thumb and finger. As the twist gets up toward the wad, it will begin to "draft" more fibers into itself and, if uncontrolled, it will gather too many and make a lump or "slub" on the thread. It is the educated control of the draft that makes a good spinster.

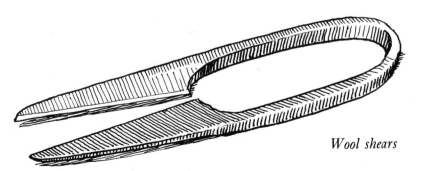
Wool shears

A hand spindle and its use

It isn't practical to spin a long continuous thread without some kind of mechanical help; only spiders can do that. The simplest aid is as old as spinning. It is the hand spindle, which was used at least three thousand years B.C. and is still used in Asia and Africa. The spindle is a tapered stick, about eight inches long, passing through a wood or clay flywheel, called the whorl, which is fixed to it a couple of inches from the thicker end. A bit of finger-twisted thread is made, wrapped a few turns on the long end of the spindle, and secured near the point with a hitch.

Then the spindle is suspended by the yarn and given a twirl. The whorl keeps it turning for quite a time, and as it turns it twists the yarn into thread. Unspun yarn is held in the right hand and the left controls the draft. When the spindle slows down, it is given a fresh start before it can begin reversing itself. When the spun yarn grows too long to be handled conveniently, it is wound on the spindle near the whorl, its end is hitched near the point, and the operation is repeated. It is easy to take a new sliver from the mass of wool held on a distaff under the left arm and work it into the end of the spun thread.

The spinning wheel in its simplest form, which was the wool wheel, was nothing more than a mechanical way of rotating a spindle. The spindle itself was exactly like the hand spindle, except that the whorl had a groove around it for a belt, and it worked in a horizontal position instead of a vertical one. The belt passed from the whorl around a large wheel that the spinster, standing by it, turned or stopped at will with her right hand, or with a wooden "wheel finger." This was a stick about nine inches long with a knob on one end so that it would readily catch a spoke. Some spinsters put a child at the job of turning the wheel.

The yarn was spun off the tip of the spindle and was held horizontally in the same axis with the spindle as it twisted. To wind finished yarn onto the spindle, the spinster moved her hand toward the wheel until the yarn was at a right angle to the spindle shaft. She gave the wheel a little push and the yarn was wound up. Sometimes a corncob was stuck on the spindle and the yarn was wound on it. The cob could be replaced when it was full without the spinster having to stop and wind yarn off.

It was eventually wound off, however, on a hand reel called a "niddy-noddy" or on pegs inserted into the spokes of the spinning wheel or, in

Spinning wool yarn

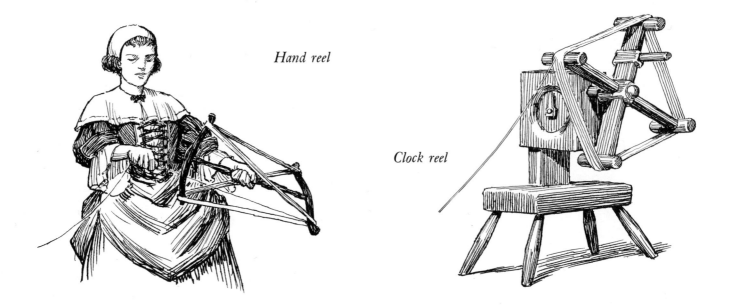

Hand reel

Clock reel

later days, on a clock reel that clicked when forty strands had been wound. Any of these systems produced forty-strand hanks, fifty-four inches around. Seven hanks (or "knots") of wool made a skein. Six skeins was a good day's spinning, at the end of which the spinster had walked miles, half of them backward.

Flax Production

Flax is tough stuff. The desirable fibers of flax lie under a tough bark and around a hard core. It took about twenty operations, all laborious, to reduce the plant to a state that would allow its fibers to be spun. Since the reader is unlikely to want to prepare any flax, not every step is detailed here.

In harvesting, the plants were yanked up by the roots, dried, and "rippled" in the field. Rippling was dragging the stalks through a coarse wooden comb to strip off the seed pods, which were saved and pressed to get linseed oil.

The rippled stalks were bundled in "bates" and "retted" (rotted) by soaking them in water under weights for five days. Retting in ponds was unpopular because it killed fish; running water was preferred. The object of retting was to make the central core of the plant brittle, so that it could be broken into short pieces on a flax brake and be more easily removed.

A flax brake was about five feet long and three feet high. Its working parts were supported on stout legs. Connecting the two end pairs of these were three or four wooden slats, set side by side on

edge. They were called "knives"; their upper edges were thinned somewhat. Opposed to these, and hinged to one end of them was another set of knives, working between the lower ones. The flax was laid across the lower knives and the upper set was brought down forcibly upon it, literally breaking the stalks but not the strong linen fiber. Sometimes a wooden mallet was used to pound the brake. It was work for men. After the flax had been put through a coarse "open" brake, it was broken again on a finer "close" brake. Then it was ready to be swingled or "scutched."

The object of swingling was to get the bark off and to remove the broken bits of core. A bundle of stalks was hung over the end of an upright board and beaten with scraping, downward strokes of a

A flax brake

Swingling, or scutching flax

Flax-Spinning

The flax wheel was invented in the sixteenth century and, aside from other advantages, it justified itself by allowing the spinster to work sitting down. The drive wheel was turned by a crank which was kept going by a treadle. The flax wheel had not one but two belts; one drove the whorl of the spindle, the other a pulley, slightly smaller than the whorl, made on the end of a bobbin that turned freely on the spindle, using it as an axle.

The spindle was an entirely different affair from the one on the wool wheel. Instead of having a point from which the thread was twisted, the flax spindle had a hollow end and the thread was twisted in that. The finished yarn made an exit through a hole in the side of the spindle (it was really the side hole that twisted the fibers) and was led to one of the hooks, on one leg or the other, of a horseshoe-shaped "flyer" that was made as part of the spindle and turned with it. From the flyer it was wound on the bobbin which, because of its smaller pulley, ran slightly faster than the spindle. Linen is strong, so the constant tension, which increased as the bobbin filled, seldom broke the thread; besides, the belt could easily be made to slip a little in the pulley groove.

From time to time bobbins had to be changed. To get one off, it was necessary to remove the spindle. This was made easy by the use, on the pulley end, of a leather bearing that was nothing more than a doubled thong, with its two ends thrust through a hole in the supporting post. Tension on the belts was controlled by turning a knob on the end of the platform; this rotated a threaded wooden rod that moved the whole spindle support.

The spinning of linen yarn was more continuous than making wool yarn. Like wool, the linen was wound off the bobbins into knots of forty threads, but a skein of linen was twenty knots, against seven for wool.

Making cloth requires quantities of spun yarn, so, when there was nothing else that had to be done, New England women and girls spun. If there was a chance to spend a day gossiping at a neighbor's, the good wife took along her baby and her spinning wheel. Sometimes, in the back country, she rode a horse with the baby on her lap and her wheel tied on behind the saddle. There may

long wooden "swingling knife." Both sides of the bundle were dealt with. This, too, was hard work and it was done twice over. A good man could swingle forty pounds of flax a day. The coarse stuff that was knocked out by the second swingling could be used for bagging.

After swingling, the flax fibers were combed out straight and cleaned of the broken fibers, called "tow," by being drawn through a series of "hetchels" with increasingly fine teeth. All this work, and the spinning that followed it, is now done by machinery, not better but much faster.

Hackling and the "hetchel" with which it was done

The flax wheel

The inset is an enlargement of the spindle, the bobbin, and the belt-tightening device, which is cut away for clarity

have been Colonial homes north of the Susquehanna that didn't own a spinning wheel, but they were few and far between.

Weaving

After the spinning was done, its product had to be woven and this, too, was done at home, on homemade looms. Linen fabric was made into clothing, napkins, and sheets; wool cloth into clothing and blankets. Together they were wōven into the universal fabric of the common man, lin-

A Colonial loom

sey-woolsey, which was a warm, woolen weft on a strong, linen warp. Until the eighteenth century cotton was an imported luxury valuable for its rarity. The "tow," with bits of bark still clinging to it, that was removed from flax in its second swingling, served to make canvas and sacking. Sometimes, spun finer, it was made into material for very scratchy shirts, work smocks (called "longshorts"), and floppy summer pants of calf-length.

All weaving is done on a base of taut, parallel threads called a warp. To make a plain fabric, a single continuous thread, called the weft, is passed back and forth across the warp threads, joining them and, at the same time, being supported by them. In any single passage across the fabric, the weft passes under alternate warp threads; on its return passage, it must pass *over* those threads and under the ones it missed on the first trip.

Since it is impractical to pick up one warp thread at a time and pass a bulky roll of weft under it, a way had to be found to raise all the odd-numbered threads at one time, allow the weft to be passed under them, and then to pick up all the even-numbered threads for the weft to be passed back under *them*. Apart from acting as a frame to hold the work, this alternating pickup is the principal purpose of a loom. The device is very ancient.

A Colonial loom was built as a rectangular framework of squared timbers, held together with mortise-and-tenon joints. The loom was big, and heavy, and strong, as it had to be to stand the strains put upon it. It stood seven feet high and took up more floor space than a double bed. The whole structure was carefully made, plumb and square. Again it *had* to be; a crooked loom weaves crooked cloth.

The warp was precut to length and stretched horizontally from back to front of the loom. At the back it was wound with infinite care on an octagonal roller that had handles for turning it, and suspended weights, or a ratchet, for braking it. This roller was called the warp beam. Warp was unwound from it as the work progressed. At the front of the loom, just short of the plank that served the weaver as a seat, the warp passed over a smooth rounded timber, called the breast beam, and then back and down to another roller, called the cloth beam, on which finished work was rolled up.

About halfway between the breast beam and the warp beam the warp passed through the heddles that did the job of picking up alternate threads to form what weavers call a shed for the weft to pass through. Modern looms usually have metal heddles, but old ones were made of strong linen string. Each thread of the warp had its own heddle, made with a loop or eye in its middle to carry the warp thread. The heddles were strung vertically, side by side, between horizontal wooden strips and the whole assembly was called a harness. Plain weaving needed two parallel harnesses, one for the odd threads, and one for the even threads.

Getting the warp onto the loom, measuring for length, avoiding tangles, getting every thread in its right place and all at even tension, was a complicated and exacting job for at least two people. Even now, with modern short cuts, half of any book on weaving is likely to be devoted to "warping." Pattern weaving was even more complex, since it required four or more harnesses. To make a pattern, arrangements had to be made for the weft to skip warp threads occasionally, and it all had to be done by the threading of the harnesses.

Most of the early Colonial production was plain weaving. The two harnesses, hanging side by side, were connected by ropes that passed over a roller

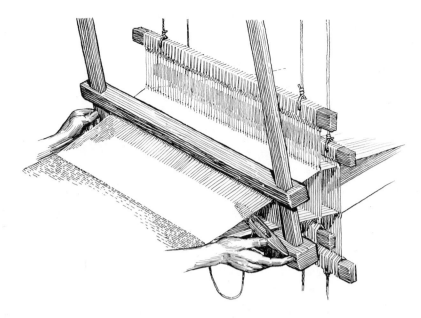

A close view of the "shed," the batten, and the harness

at the top of the loom. If one harness was pulled down, the other had to rise, carrying with it only its own warp threads; those of the other harness slipped, unaffected, between the heddles of the rising harness. The harnesses were moved up and down by the alternate pressure of the weaver's feet on two treadles. These were hinged at the back of the loom and were connected to the bottoms of the harnesses by nicely adjusted ropes.

Between the weaver and the heddles was the swinging batten, pivoted at the top of the loom and hanging by two wooden side pieces called swords. The batten itself was made of two heavy pieces of wood, one above the warp and one below. Fixed between them was the reed, a comb-like affair, originally made with slivers of actual reed closely and evenly spaced. The warp threads passed between the reeds, which were tall enough to allow space for the rise and fall of the shed. This was necessary because the actual weaving was done in *front* of the reed and, after every pass of the shuttle, the batten was pulled forward to pound the weft firmly into place. The thump of the batten was a familiar sound in American homes for two centuries.

In action, the weaver raised one harness and threw the boat-shaped wooden shuttle so that it slid through the shed, from hand to hand, trailing its yarn behind it. The shed was then closed, the batten was swung forward and back again, the other shed was opened, and the hand that had

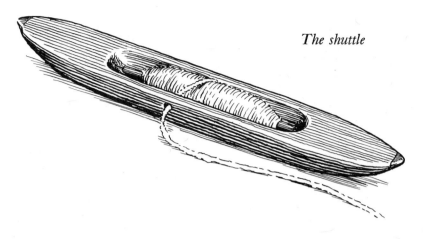

The shuttle

caught the shuttle threw it back again. A hard-working skilled weaver could make about three yards of thirty-inch-wide cloth a day with heavy wool yarn. Most looms made cloth no wider than thirty inches because it was hard to throw a shuttle farther than that and still catch it.

The shuttle was about eight inches long and was made of hard close-grained wood. Boxwood was favored in England; over here dogwood was found to be a perfect substitute and applewood was sometimes used. Since the shuttle was thrown in both directions, its bluntly pointed ends were identical and usually were tipped with metal to guard them from accidents.

There was a recess cut into the shuttle, large enough to hold the quill, from which the weft thread unwound, making its exit through a hole in the shuttle's side. Quills were wound in advance, of course. Some actual feather quills were used; more often they were short pieces of hollow reed. Paper ones are now used. The quill rotated on a wire that was sprung into holes made for it in the ends of the shuttle recess.

The weaver worked sitting on a bench that was part of the loom, "suspended between heaven and earth," one wrote. Both hands and feet were constantly busy and, every now and again, it was necessary to get down, release a few inches of warp, and take up a corresponding amount on the cloth beam. Weaving seems to have been a soothing and satisfying occupation. Though spinning

The quill

was exclusively a woman's task, it wasn't considered effeminate for a man to weave. In time there came to be professional weavers, men who traveled through the country, like the soap-and-candle-makers, weaving yarn spun in the household and using the household's loom for the job.

Clothing

Up to the middle of the century, New England clothes were sober and restrained; even the wealthy, though their garments might be rich, wore little in the way of ornament. The elders were in control and everybody, Puritan or not, dressed as they ordained. In the second half of the century, more and more people in the towns wore fine clothes and aped the fashions of London, regardless of the thunderbolts hurled at them from the meetinghouses.

Clothing was issued to the original settlers who landed at Salem and the list of what they received has been preserved. For the men, jerkins and doublets of leather are mentioned. The difference between the two is slight and, at this date, a little vague. Both were outer garments worn as we wear coats. The jerkin was likely to be a sleeveless pullover, with a short slit at the neck in front. The doublet may actually have been of double thickness; that's how it got its name originally. It was open all the way down the front and was fastened with hooks-and-eyes, loops, or points. Buttons existed, but were thought to be a "vanity" by the early Puritans, as they still are by the Amish. The button taboo lasted only a few years in New England; before thirty years had passed even the elders wore buttons galore, and other, vainer furbelows as well.

Points were rows of short strings or tapes, attached to opposite edges of a garment; they were simply tied together. They were used in various places and on different kinds of clothes. The ends of the strings were finished with metal tags or with tassels. Breeches were usually held up by being tied to the doublet with points. Doublets usually had sleeves, or were provided with points around the armholes so that sleeves could be tied on; non-Puritans might use buttons for this. Seventeenth-century sleeves were frequently separate garments.

Loops were set in a row also, but on one edge

Puritans in
Sunday-go-to-meeting clothes.
The man on the left wears
a jerkin, he on the right, a doublet under
his cloak, the one in the middle has a cassock on and has his feet in clogs

only. Opposite each loop was a hole like a button-hole. Fastening was accomplished by passing the bottom loop through its hole and then passing the next loop through its hole *and* through the loop that projected from the hole below, and so on up to the neck, where there was a string to tie the top loop.

Leather breeches are mentioned in the Salem list. These were baggy and tied below the knee, as all breeches were. The stockings below them were knitted from wool or tailored from cloth or leather. Breeches became tighter after a while, but leather ones, made from deer hide or sheepskin, continued to be worn by most workingmen and farmers until the beginning of the nineteenth century. They were so universally worn that they came to be made by specialists who turned out nothing else.

In cold weather, when we would wear an over-coat, the settlers wore cloaks or cassocks. The cas-sock was the more nearly like an overcoat because it had sleeves; otherwise it was a loose smocklike affair. A cloak was a cape; usually it was provided with a strip of cloth that the wearer could fasten across his throat, to keep the cloak on when it was thrown back. Whether they were intended to be worn by men or women, cloaks often had hoods. A woman's riding hood was really a hooded cape. It and other cloaks were more often scarlet than any other color.

The caps issued at Salem were scarlet; each man got two of them. They might have been the same kind of flat "city" cap that can be seen in the paintings of Holbein but, more probably (and more practically), they were high at the rear, with short brims in front and turned-up flaps on back and sides that could be pulled down when needed to cover the ears. Their descendants are still worn for farm work and hunting.

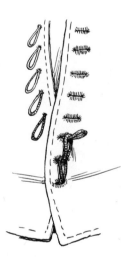

Loops

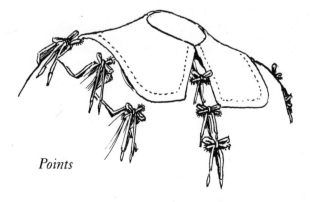

Points

Flat "city" cap

Ear-flapped "Monteiro" cap

Children were dressed exactly like their elders, once they emerged from babyhood. That period was considered to last until they were about six years old and in it both boys and girls wore "petticoats," sometimes confusingly called "coats," "pinners" (aprons), and "hanging sleeves." These last were extra sleeves, not intended to cover the arms but attached at the shoulders and almost reaching the ground. They served the purpose of "handles" with which to assist a child in learning to walk. They were worn a far longer time than any practical need required and were a badge of childhood, detested by their older wearers. The little girl standing by the Puritan dinner table is wearing them.

Women's skirts were all called petticoats. Sometimes they wore several at the same time, one over another. The uppermost was often caught up in some way, in front, in front and back, or on both sides. The feminine doublet which was correct in 1630 was soon replaced by the bodice, called at first a "pair of bodies" and looking like an outside corset, laced front and back. Some kind of bodice was worn by nearly all women for more than a century. For quite as long they all wore hoods; if a hat was worn, it went on over the hood. A woman who was a widow, and more were then than now, wore a little cap with a point in the front, the "widow's peak," just showing under her hood.

The names of some standard garments have changed: pants (breeches) were once hose, skirts were petticoats, a petticoat (or something like it) was a shift, a lounging robe was a nightgown, a nightgown was a rail. House slippers were made of felt and were called slip shoes or slips; anyone so slovenly as to wear them outdoors was, of course, slipshod. Some things have vanished entirely: a rochet, for instance, was a woman's three-cornered mantle, red in winter, white in summer. What man wears spatterdashes nowadays to keep his clothes clean when he rides horseback? They were loose thigh-high leggings. For the same purpose, women wore stirrup stockings, two yards wide at the top, in which they could crowd their petticoats and their modesty and ride astride. For riding pillion, there was an overskirt, called a "safe-

Puritan women.
On left: a head rail, widow's peak,
woman's doublet, and looped petticoat.
Second figure: laced "bodies."
Third: a riding hood.
On right: hat over hood,
and a rochet over a doublet

54

Stirrup stockings.
Perhaps the least attractive of all female garments

guard," that could be removed and tied to the saddle while in church.

Rubber shoes were unknown until quite recent times, of course, but mud has long been with us. Men too poor for boots wore wooden-soled clogs over their shoes to walk in mud. Clogs were made like modern scuffs, open at the back. There were clogs for women and for children too, but many women preferred pattens. These also had wooden soles and were worn over other shoes, but they had a back to the heel and a strap across the instep, and the entire sole was elevated an inch or so above a flat iron ring that was in contact with the ground. They weren't easy to walk in; an old diarist complains of his wife's slowness in them. At about the end of the seventeenth century (maybe they were older than that) loose canvas boots with short tops and wooden soles were called "golo-shoes." Something like them is still worn under the name of galoshes.

Towns and Discipline

New England is made up of small farms clustered around small towns. It grew that way from its earliest days. The land was divided into fairly large sections called townships, and subdivided into farms, or "freeholds." With a church as a nucleus, a village was started in each township and, to govern the whole section, a town meeting was set up. Every voter had an equal voice in the meeting, but to vote a man had to own land and had also to be a church member. It wasn't democracy, but it was the egg from which democracy was hatched. Only in Rhode Island, and there only in its early years, did *every* man have a vote.

The church was the center of everything; everybody, member or not, Puritan or not, had to attend if he could stand up and put one foot ahead of the other. Because expulsion from the church meant the loss of one's vote, and because the preacher could dictate who should be thrown out, the clergy were in full political control. They didn't hesitate to "try" and condemn from the pulpit and to impose sentence for minor offenses.

The meetinghouse stood facing an open lot, the common, so called because it was common property and any townsman might graze his livestock there. Often the common was of considerable size, far larger than it appears in the illustration.

In 1630 there were only three cows in New England, but the number was steadily increased and sheep and swine were added. The commons became inadequate and town herdsmen were appointed who took care of everybody's cows on other common lands outside the town. At first the owners brought them to a meeting place each morning and collected them at night; then the cows caught on and had only to be turned loose at sunrise and to have the stable door left open for them in the evening. In the autumn, pigs were taken to the woods by a swineherd, to fatten on beechnuts and acorns before they were turned into bacon and lard.

Houses stood all around the common and were built back from it, when all the space had been taken up. The preacher lived in the best house; the others were occupied by tradesmen and artisans and sometimes by farmers whose land was near-by.

Next to the meetinghouse there was a long building known as the Sabbath house. It was divided in half. One end was a stable, the other a large room with a fireplace. Here country people who had come to meeting could shelter their horses, cook their dinner, and warm up at midday. There was no heat in the church except from a few hot coals you might carry in a metal foot warmer, which didn't last through the four-hour sermon. And that was only the morning session; there was another in the afternoon.

The Puritans had a mighty consciousness of sin and found themselves forever punishing somebody. Ordinary humans had to break out somewhere, and the low and the high did so. They used bad language; they got drunk; they committed outrageous immoralities. If they were caught, they were very publicly punished. The basis of Puritan punishment was humiliation. Minor transgressors were locked in the stocks, or the pillory, with some sign of their fault hung upon them where all could see it: a large "D" for the drunkard, a "B" for the blasphemer who, if he blasphemed sulphurously enough, might also find his tongue in a cleft stick.

More drastic and cruel things were done, but it isn't to be thought that cruel punishments were exclusively Puritan; they were customary in all of the Colonies, though perhaps it was easier to incur them in New England. Flesh was branded with hot iron; ears were cut off and so were hands, always with the idea that the criminal should be marked and humiliated.

The stocks, the pillory, and the whipping post usually stood in front of the meetinghouse. There was logic in that; it was the chief gathering place of the people. To the door of the meetinghouse were tacked all public notices of new laws, of sales, banns of marriage, and town meetings. Nailed on the walls of the building were the heads of predatory animals on which bounties had been paid. A Puritan meetinghouse was not in itself sacred; it was merely a place of assembly. It was the center of social life, the source of news, and the exchange where business was done. Even on the Sabbath a little quiet trading was done between sermons, this in spite of the fact that it was written of a Puritan, at the time, that "he hanged his cat on Monday, for killing of a mouse on Sunday."

A late seventeenth-century New England village.
This is a composite drawing. The meeting house is at the extreme left

Trades and Crafts

Naturally the villages were the centers of business for their own townships and, as such, they attracted craftsmen in special trades, who usually throve. In later days New England towns sometimes advertised the opportunities they offered for a needed craftsman. A cooper was of prime importance and so was a tanner and a miller. The same stream that turned the gristmill might also run the sawmill. Along the coast, power for these was sometimes obtained by putting a gated dam across an inlet. The gate was closed at high tide, trapping the water and holding it until the tide fell; then the water was released to turn a mill wheel as it ran back to the sea.

All of the metal workers did well. The blacksmith not only made horseshoes and oxshoes and applied them, he was also a notable maker of hardware. Latches, hinges, andirons, "cob" irons (a single bar, with feet, used in place of andirons),

spits, rushlight holders, farm tools, even nails, he made by hand—and most of them were handsome. Bog-iron ore was found and, because the need was great, small foundries were started for smelting it. The earliest one at Saugus, Massachusetts, was begun in 1646. England encouraged her colonies to produce pig iron but did all she could to keep them from making anything from it, with the idea of protecting her ironworkers at home.

The blacksmith used charcoal to heat metal. A modern ironworker uses coal in his forge and forces air into the fire with a motor-driven fan; the Colonial blacksmith blew his fire with an enormous bellows that required a couple of deerskins, or a whole bull's hide, to make. It was the job of an apprentice to pump the bellows and keep the fire hot.

Everything was made by hand, of course, so every manufactured article was unique. If it was a chair, there might be other chairs of its kind but

57

The blacksmith and his apprentice

there was no other *exactly* like it. After the purchaser of such a product had owned it a while, especially if it had been made to his personal specifications, its characteristics revealed themselves and the familiar thing became *his* in a sense far stronger than a mass-produced article, one of ten million, can ever be ours.

The whitesmith, who made things of tin (tin-plated sheet iron, that is), wasn't supposed to be able to do much except repair work. The British wouldn't send any unfabricated sheet metal over. They wanted to sell their own finished tinware. This took the form of candleholders, tinderboxes, foot warmers, "lanthornes," and various dippers and strainers for cookery. Somehow the Yankees got sheet tin, however. Perhaps they rolled it themselves. They are known to have shipped tinware to the South in the seventeenth century.

The pewterer was in trouble. He needed tin, copper, and lead. All three were scarce, and no native tin was found at all. As a result all American pewterware for many years was made by reworking discarded articles that originally had been made in England. Silversmiths didn't appear until the seventeenth century was nearly over and then only in big towns like Boston. Few people in

Butterfly hinge

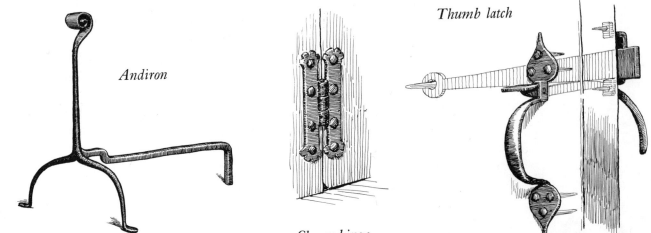

Andiron

Clover hinge

Thumb latch

Blacksmith's work

Joiner's work.
Gateleg table

Chest

early days had wealth enough to buy "plate," as they called it.

The joiner hadn't the metalworker's troubles in getting material for the sturdy furniture he made. As men grew more prosperous, they were glad to pay for better bedsteads than they could knock together themselves at home. Their wives, too, demanded lighter and better-looking stuff: chairs with turned legs; chests with drawers that fitted; drop-leaf tables that would store in a little space and expand at need; and ornamental paneling

around the fireplace to cover some of the rough stone.

The joiner wasn't called a cabinetmaker until after 1700, but of course he was one. His hand tools were the same ones that are used in his trade today, except that only the actual cutting parts of them were metal. The bits of his planes were held in their wooden blocks by wooden wedges, those of his small augers by wooden thumbscrews. His tools would do anything modern tools will do, but not so fast.

Spring-pole lathe

Whitesmith's work.
Lanthorne and sconce

The cobbler

worker develops a steady rhythm and hardly knows he is pausing. Turners used lathes also. They made bowls, cups, and round trenchers of wood.

The cobbler always made a living. The most constant human occupation is wearing out shoe leather and, in a day when most people walked almost everywhere they went, it wore out faster. We are told that walking a thirty-mile round trip to town was no great matter. If the cobbler was good, he was also a cordwainer, that is he not only mended shoes, he made them, too. The uppers of all shoes were hand-sewn, and so were the soles of some, but heavy soles and all heels were put on with wooden pegs. The shoemaker didn't have to bother with matching a pair of shoes as mates, right and left; he merely made two shoes, exactly alike. Either shoe could be worn, with more or less comfort, on either foot.

The widespread custom of wearing homemade clothes limited the demand for the tailor's services, but he was to be found in the larger centers, with an increasing number of his kind, perched on his curious two-story bench. Tailors also worked sitting cross-legged on a table. Either way the idea was to keep the work off the floor, which was likely to be dirty, anywhere except in New Netherland. Like the cobbler, the tailor did all of his sewing by hand, because there wasn't any other way for him to do it. A machine that could sew would, for him, have involved witchcraft. Most custom tailors now work for men; the Colonial tailor worked for the

There was no motor to run his lathe. He powered it with his own leg and he could rotate his "stuff," as he called his work, only in intermittent spurts. A strong cord was carried straight up from the foot treadle of the lathe, around the stuff (one turn), and was attached to the free end of a springy pole, fastened near the ceiling. The work itself was free to turn on metal centers inserted in its ends. Pressing down on the treadle spun the stuff against the chisel and bent the pole downward. Releasing the pressure at the bottom of the stroke allowed the pole to pull the cord up again, and work paused until the treadle had recovered. In practice this is handier than it sounds. The

The tailor

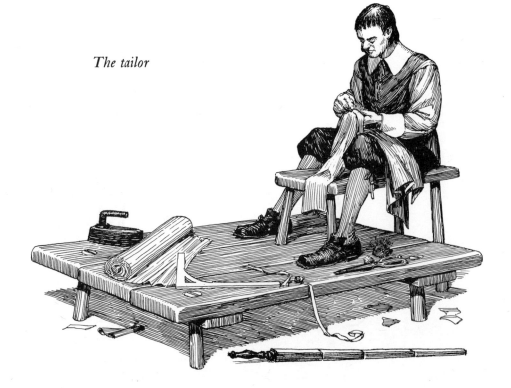

whole family and the servants. Not infrequently he remade clothes, cutting down Father's old britches to fit Sonny. Bills have turned up that attest these facts; many of them mention by name the members of the family for whom work was done.

Travel and Mail

In Boston and in a few of the larger towns inns were established, but outlying villages couldn't support them. Usually in these some householder was given tax concessions, or an actual subsidy, to persuade him (or, more likely, her, for it was often undertaken by a widow) to maintain an ordinary, since there was no profit in it otherwise. An ordinary was in a sense an inn; a traveler could get a bed, a meal, and food for his horse, if he had one. It offered the plainest of accommodation and the guest was expected to eat whatever he was offered, though it might be corn-meal mush, and often was.

As travelers became more numerous, some of the ordinaries prospered into real inns and, adding a bar, became the secular gathering places for their townships. In them mail was received and held, lying on a table, until it was found by its addressee or by someone who was willing to carry a letter to him.

A letter was written on paper made by hand from linen rags, with a pen, hand-cut from the quill of a goose or a wild turkey, dipped in ink, homemade from vinegar and ox gall or from tea and iron. The ink was blotted by scattering dry sand over the page and then pouring the sand back into its container. The knife that converted a quill into a pen was, naturally, a penknife. We have kept the name and apply it to what our forefathers called a jackknife; penknives were small. The whole equipment was kept in a desk, which wasn't a piece of furniture to which you might draw up a chair, but was a small box, often with a slanted lid convenient for writing when the desk was put on a table.

Letters were not then, or for years afterward, enclosed in envelopes. Instead the sheets were folded so that none of the writing could be seen, and were sealed with a blob of hot wax into which the writer impressed his seal from an engraved disk with a handle or from his signet ring. The address was written directly on the sealed packet. Addresses had to be descriptive. Since there were no street numbers, a town address usually located the addressee's house by a near-by landmark, often a tavern or shop sign, as: *To Mr. Faithfull Freeman, near the sign of the Plow, in Milk Street, Boston.* Signs were useful because they had pictures on them or were carved to represent something, and so could be identified by the many people who couldn't read. There was no postal service. Letters

The "Blue Anchor" inn

Ride and tie

the Puritan temperament. It's said that an Indian could usually buy back, for almost nothing, a canoe he had sold to a New Englander. Goodman Stiffback couldn't keep the thing right side up!

The only roads at first were the paths the Indians had made through the forests. These were all right for walking and passable on horseback, but they were too narrow for any kind of vehicle. The early scarcity of horses bred the ingenious system of ride-and-tie, by which two men could gain some advantage from one horse without exhausting him by making him carry double. One would mount and ride ahead, the other would start walking. When the rider had covered an agreed distance, he tied the horse and continued on foot. When the first pedestrian reached the horse, he mounted and rode on *past* the original rider to the next tying point, where he walked on again. All three had some rest.

Hauling was done with oxcarts and they needed roads of some width. The first ones were the "mast roads" that were made to get timber for the British Navy out of the woods. These went straight to where they were going, with no nonsense, but they seldom went where anybody wanted to go. The township roads were different. Their destinations

were entrusted to someone, or passed from hand to hand, for delivery.

Along the coast and up the rivers, travel was by boat, and that was by far the easiest way to get places but it wasn't always possible. Fat-bellied shallops were used. There is one in the illustration of the Newtown ferry. Canoes didn't seem to suit

A gate on a township road

were all right, but their routes were not. They had no legal status. Each man whose land they crossed owned his part of them. He gated them where he wished and bent them around his fields as he pleased. Travel on them was slow.

All New England roads lead eventually to the sea. Almost as soon as they were opened a flow of products for export began to move down them. Most of these products were carried in American ships. "A prodigious ship of 300 Tons" was built at Salem in 1641 and it was but the first of an unbroken succession that continued until steam took over the oceans. The supply of timber seemed unlimited, so costs were low and even in the seventeenth century English owners began to have ships built in Massachusetts.

In Boston and Salem, shipowners and merchants became established and waxed prosperous, importing manufactured articles that were needed in the Colony and exporting lumber, furs, and salt fish. Most of the trade was with England, and the British wanted all of it to be, but the Yankees were soon trading with the other Colonies and with the West Indies. When Britain tried to enforce restrictions on trade, smuggling became a respectable occupation, not only in New England but all down the coast.

Every ship had on board a man known as the supercargo; officially he was the businessman of the ship and represented the owners, unofficially he performed private commissions for individuals. These included purchases overseas and also conveying and selling consignments of home products gathered together in a community. Miss Abigail's pickles and Brother Jonathon's shingles traveled together as a small trading venture.

Education

Among the original Puritan settlers there were a few men who had been to college and quite a number who could read, so it isn't surprising that attention was paid to education, though it's startling to realize that they started Cambridge College (Harvard) only *six* years after they landed. The answer lies in the need to train ministers. To judge from the list of thirty-nine books presented to the College by Governor Winthrop, the higher education of the time was dry stuff. A president of Harvard wrote to one of the Governor's descend-

Supercargo checking the lading of a ship

ants in 1849 ". . . I think I may congratulate you that your honored ancestor did not transmit them [the books] to you."

The College received twelve pence a year and a peck of corn from every family in the Colony and, in addition, had the revenue of the ferry that was established between Newtown (Charlestown) and Boston. This ferry carried people only, in a small boat; if you had a horse he had to swim behind.

Many children had to learn as they could at home, but some towns had dame schools, where children were taught the cathechism, the Lord's Prayer, and incidentally the alphabet, from the time-honored hornbook. This was a little frame

The Newtown ferry

with a handle on it. A piece of paper with the alphabet printed on one side and the Lord's Prayer on the other was slipped into the frame between two pieces of horn, scraped so thin as to be dimly transparent. Sometimes paper and horn were merely tacked to a paddle, as in the illustration. When the letters were drawn directly on the wood, and left unprotected, the paddle was known as a battledore.

The ancient Anglo-Saxon letter called "thorn," printed as "y" but pronounced as "th," was still in use in the seventeenth century. When Stephen Daye and other Colonials printed "ye" for the definite article, they and their readers pronounced it "the," just as you do. So, too, the long "ess" (f) that looked like an "eff" (f). It appeared anywhere a small "s" would now be used, except at the end of a word, but "feffions" was never pronounced any way but as "sessions."

Lessons were often written in doggerel rhyme as an aid to memory. One of these is still familiar to most people: "Thirty days hath September . . ." Sometimes scholars had scraps of paper, more often written lessons had to be done on birch bark with a "plummet" of lead, real lead, not the graphite called lead that we use in pencils. If handled gently, birch bark serves quite well as paper.

Town schools were set up by law in Massachusetts after 1647, but some were started by private subscribers before that. One of these is still in existence, the Roxbury Latin School, founded in 1645 by that John Eliot who translated the Bible into the Indian language. In its early days, Roxbury was a one-room school where books were so scarce and so valuable that scholars were required to handle them with "thumb papers." The curriculum concentrated on Latin and the preparation for Latin. It was the language of learning; Harvard students had to recite in Latin and were supposed to converse in it also! Most Roxbury pupils gave up when they had completed the preparation, a reasonably solid grounding in the three R's, and the much-valued ability to "do sums."

II. NEW NETHERLAND

FUR WAS "BEING WORN" in Europe in the early seventeenth century and it had always been popular in Russia, so the Dutch colony in America went into the fur business and prospered from the start. Hatters found that the felt they could make from the underfur, or muffoon, of the beaver was better for their purpose than anything made from rabbit, or wool, or even from otter or muskrat. Old fur that had been worn until it was dirty and greasy made the best felt. That created a market for the filthy "matchcoats" (*matchigotes*) that Indians had worn and discarded. In time beaver skins that had been sold to the Russians and worn to rags were repurchased in western

Europe and made into hats. A beaver hat would last fifty years and was so expensive that a man often made a special bequest of his hat in his will.

Hat-Making

Beaver hats were soon made in the Colonies as well as in Europe. The first step in turning beaver skins into hats was to pluck the fur off the hides. This was done with the thumb, pressing against a flat slip of bone or wood held in the hand and backed by the forefinger. It is stated that the soft underfur was removed and the coarse "guard hairs" were left attached, as they grew. Lacking firsthand knowledge, one must accept this as true; practiced skill can accomplish remarkable things.

In order to mat the fur into a fabric, it was necessary to rearrange the fibers, mixing them up so that they crisscrossed one another. For this the fur was piled on a special table with turned-up ends, and "bowed." The taut catgut string of a six-foot wooden bow was passed repeatedly through the pile and twanged with a knobbed plectrum as it passed. The vibration of the string did the mixing. The natural barbs on the hairs made them cling together.

Loose mixed fur was patted into a flat triangle called a bat. It had rounded corners, and each side of it was eighteen inches or more long. The bats

were dampened and a number of them were stacked with cloth separators between them. The entire stack was kneaded by hand to start compacting the fur into felt. At the end of this operation the bats had shrunk one third. By introducing separators slightly smaller than the bats, it was possible to intermingle the fur fibers along two sides of a pair of bats, felting them together into a conical unit known as a hood. This was the first step in forming the felt into a hat, but before the next step was taken the hoods were further shrunk and compacted by fulling, that is, soaking them in a very hot, slightly acid solution. After soaking, the hood was rolled around a wooden rod and further kneaded or even pounded.

Shaping was done by stretching and pressing the boiling-hot wet hood over a wooden mold. The hatter avoided scalding his hands by constantly dipping them in cold water. Some molds included the brim, but most of them shaped the crown only. The brim was ordinarily formed by hand and trimmed to size. The molded hat was dried overnight in a warm oven and, in the morning, was finished by smoothing it with pumice or fine sandpaper. If the hat was to have a nap, as all good beaver hats had, it was raised, after smoothing, by working over the surface with a fine scratcher, made like a wool card.

The main sources of beaver pelts were New

Hatters

Dutch houses in New Amsterdam

Netherland and New France. The Dutch West India Company, sponsors of the New Netherland settlement, naturally tried to hold a monopoly of the Colony's fur trade, and did handle most of it, but there was considerable smuggling. The Dutch *boschlopers* (woods-runners) went into the forests and traded forbidden rum and firearms for furs; and a considerable amount of "kitchen trading" was done by the outlying homesteaders.

Fort Orange (Albany) was the collecting point for pelts but New Amsterdam, to which they and the increasing farm products had to be sent for shipment, soon became the principal town and it has remained so.

New Netherland flourished until 1664, long enough to make the whole Hudson Valley, and half of Long Island, thoroughly Dutch. Then the English sailed in and took it over from peg-legged Peter Stuyvesant, just as he had taken over New Sweden. Stuyvesant, speechless and purple-faced with rage, was prevented by the sensible burghers from putting up a hopeless resistance and he stumped off to his farm. From then on, except for a short lapse, the Colony was officially English, but its inhabitants were still Dutch and, even now, their traces persist.

Houses

As soon as they could manage it, the settlers built themselves houses exactly like those they had lived in at home. Most of them were brick, or frame with brick ends, and their roofs were thatched at first. Later, when constant fires forced a change, they had roofs covered with curved red tiles. These were true Dutch houses, built in the towns and on farms up the Hudson. They were high and narrow. When they were built along a street, a gable end faced it, not a side wall. The roofs didn't project over the end walls, as roofs ordinarily do. Instead the wall was carried a little above the roof and was finished in a series of steps. The Dutch were much given to ornament, so the red brick of their gable ends was usually patterned with black bricks; sometimes dates and initials were built into the wall with them. The end walls were often tied to the interior timber construction with long iron rods, ending in decorative "anchoring irons" visible on the outside.

Roofs were of steep pitch and often very tall, allowing space in them for a floor of sleeping quarters, with an attic above, and a "cockloft" above that. The early roofs had no windows in them; all light and ventilation came from the

66

ends. The windows in the lower part of the house were likely to be divided into four parts by wooden mullions, and each quarter had a leaded sash of diamond or square panes. The entire window could be covered with solid wooden shutters, hung on wrought-iron hinges.

The door of a New Netherland house was almost invariably a Dutch door, made in two sections, top and bottom, hinged separately. This kind of door allowed ventilation on a warm day without inviting into the house the pigs, geese, and hens that roamed the street. The door had a big brass knocker. Diedrich Knickerbocker stretched the truth when he said a Dutch *huys vrouw* would wear out several knockers in a lifetime of daily polishing.

Two benches were customarily built outside, on either side of the door, not on the ground but on a low brick or wood platform called the *stoep*. We have inherited word and platform as "stoop." Here on pleasant evenings every family sat, the men smoking, the women knitting, and the children, beyond doubt, giggling. All who passed, friends or strangers, were expected to stop and chat a moment, or an hour.

In the countryside around New Amsterdam, the Flemish built another kind of house entirely, following the pattern of those *they* had left behind. Modern houses copied from them are miscalled "Dutch." Many of these houses were stone, though on Long Island, where there are no stones bigger than baseballs, they were of frame construction, with the outside walls covered with shingles or clapboard. Where the Dutch houses were tall and steep, the Flemish houses were a story and a half, squat and quiet. The roofs had a gentle pitch that became still flatter at the eaves, where it extended three or four feet over the building's side walls.

These houses originally had a kind of fireplace that to the modern mind seems weird. The fire was built on a dirt hearth against one wall, which was protected at that point with brick. The smoke went up through a large hole in the ceiling, into a "hood," or chamber, built in the attic of clay-smeared wood. From the hood, the smoke escaped through the roof by a small and quite normal chimney. The hood was used as a place to hang smoked meat, since the smoke would preserve it. In later houses a brick closet was built in the attic, as part of the chimney, or sometimes smoke was diverted into a large hogshead, called the smoke-house.

Inside the Houses

The principal characteristic of a New Netherland interior was its spotless cleanliness. The Dutch passion for constant cleaning seemed eccentric to visitors from the English Colonies, where no such habit prevailed. Even unpainted woodwork and the beams across ceilings are reported by visitors to have been scoured to whiteness, though many Dutch houses had whitewashed walls and ceilings. Floors were scrubbed and sprinkled with clean sand, which can't have been very pleasant to walk on. Window glass sparkled at all times, and fresh linen curtains were hung weekly.

A Flemish farmhouse in New Netherland

*The making of a birch broom
and the finished product*

New England as well. As late as 1820 a birch broom could be bought in towns for six cents.

The material for a broom was a six-foot birch log five inches thick. The bark was removed and fourteen inches of the butt was reduced to fine slivers with a jackknife. The upper ends of the slivers weren't detached. Then, starting at a point, say thirty inches up from the original butt, more slivers were whittled, downward this time, leaving their *lower* ends attached. This second slivering was stopped when it had reached a core the right thickness for a handle. This core was continued to the top by removing all excess wood above the whittling. The upper slivers were bent down over the lower ones and lashed in place with a few turns of swingling tow. The result was a fine broom when it had been trimmed a little.

Dutch furniture was as stout and sturdy as the people who used it, but it was seldom of home manufacture, and it was never plain. The Dutch carved and ornamented wherever they could; and they liked bright, cheerful colors. Chairs and stools had rush or leather seats and elaborately turned, bulbous legs, as did tables, also. Carved blanket chests, similar to the Puritan ones, were in use, but there was nothing in New England like the ponderous *kas,* or wardrobe, that served instead of closets or wall pegs to hold clothing.

A customary wedding present was a "garnish" of pewter, a set of plates and porringers in various sizes. These were kept highly polished by rubbing them with wood ashes and oil, and they were kept

When a Dutch housewife needed a broom she bought it or had it made by her husband, depending on where she lived. In either case it might be a common besom of hemlock twigs lashed around a handle, or the much better birch-splint broom that the Indians had invented. The making of a good birch broom took three evenings at the fireside. The production of these brooms became a rural home industry in upper New York, and in

The family room in a Dutch house

where they could be seen, along with the blue-and-white delftware owned by every household that could afford it. These things were displayed on the piece of furniture that we still call a Dutch cupboard. In addition to the pewter and delft, prosperous families usually displayed a few pieces of Holland-made silver, a couple of tankards, a porringer or two (a porringer was a bowl with one flat handle), and perhaps a sugar box with two compartments, one for lumps and one for powdered sugar. Silver attested to the solvency of the family, and it was a good way to keep extra guilders when there were no banks.

In any prosperous home there was always a "best room," a show place scrubbed every week but used only for guests, weddings, christenings, and funerals. It was a parlor, but it had a bed in it. The idea of the parlor spread later over the whole northern part of the country, and there are still rooms, full of dead air and lonely furniture, that are kept dark, week after week, so as not to fade the carpet.

A Southern visitor to New Amsterdam said that one might go all through a Dutch house without ever seeing a bed. He was quite right, but the beds were there. They were built into alcoves, closed off from the rooms by curtains or by folding doors. Not only were the beds concealed in the daytime, they were also closed up at night and some people made a habit of going to bed and locking themselves in! In one family there's a tradition of a great-grandfather who did so into the nineteenth century. It was customary to sleep on a deep feather bed, into which one sank in a way that would scandalize a modern orthopedist. On cold nights a second feather bed was used as a cover.

Cooking and Eating

An open fire was used for cooking, as was done everywhere. The typical Dutch fireplace was very

A New Netherland alcove bed

high and wasn't deeply recessed into the wall. It was often bordered with blue-and-white tiles picturing Biblical subjects. The smoke rose into a projecting canopy that was only a little lower than the ceiling but led directly into the chimney. It was customary to drape the canopy with a ruffled linen valance, a fresh one every Sunday.

The utensils for cooking were the same as those used elsewhere, with only the addition of long-handled, hinged waffle irons. Buttered waffles appealed to the Dutch and they were much given to sweet cakes and various doughnuts and crullers fried in deep fat. Their *olijkoeck*, a doughnut with apples, citron, and raisins, sounds like a thing worth reviving.

As it had with all the colonists in America, Indian corn became a staple of diet. Corn meal boiled in milk made *suppawn* or hasty pudding. Samp porridge was meal with pork or beef and various root vegetables added. It was cooked slowly for three days. By then it had formed such a thick

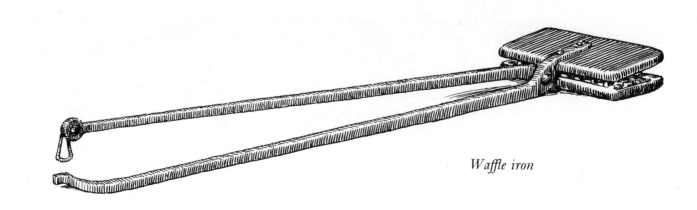

Waffle iron

Passenger pigeon.
An adult male was seventeen inches long

crust on its outside that it could be taken out of the pot in one chunk.

Such quantities of game as North America then offered probably exist nowhere in the world to-day. The passenger pigeon traveled in flocks which, even years later, so reliable an observer as Audubon estimated at over a billion birds. There were so many that their passing could be smelled and, roosting, they broke large trees. Not one survives. Venison and wild turkey could be bought in New Amsterdam for pennies. There are credible reports of foot-long oysters and six-foot lobsters in the harbor there. Shad were so plentiful that they were deemed inferior and people were embarrassed to be caught eating them. It is of interest that they still run in the Hudson and are caught within sight of the sky-scrapers.

It isn't surprising that the Hollanders over here made and ate quantities of cheese. They usually grated it, in the belief that the flavor was improved. They buttered bread, which the English at that time did not. There were public bakers in New Amsterdam in 1656 or earlier. This is known from the ordinances that regulated their prices.

Much beer, wine, and brandy were drunk daily and drunkenness was far from unknown. It was customary to furnish workmen, building a house, with libations to keep them contented; and the liquor was a substantial part of the building cost. When a man married he laid in, if he could afford it, a "pipe" of Madeira. This wine was broached at his wedding feast, then laid aside to be opened again for the christening of his first son; what was left of the 126-gallon pipe was kept to be drunk by his friends at his funeral!

Grain

Henry Hudson reported the Hudson Valley as rich farm land when he first saw it. The Dutch settlers used it for raising grain. We read of barley straw seven feet high, and of bumper crops of wheat raised, on the same ground, eleven years in succession. Tobacco-growing was introduced by some Virginians about 1635 and everybody wanted to rush into it and get rich; but the wise West India Company ruled that there must be an acre of grain raised for every acre of tobacco. They thus saved the soil and maintained a solid prosperity.

There was no farm machinery. Ripe grain had to be cut by hand with a sickle, a scythe, or a cradle, then tied in bundles and hauled to a barn, where it could be kept dry for later threshing. Only a sickle could be used in a field that still had stumps in it. A seventeenth-century sickle, though it was similar in shape to a modern one and

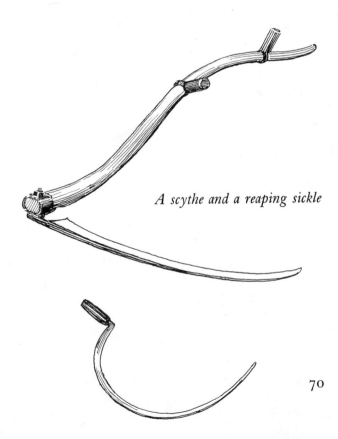

A scythe and a reaping sickle

70

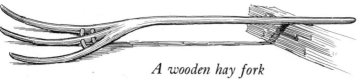

A wooden hay fork

Reaping with a cradle

intended for use with one hand only, was considerably larger than its descendant and far handsomer. A scythe was, and still is, swung with both arms. Its three-foot blade projects sideways (one can't say at a right angle) from the end of an artfully double-curved snath of wood on which are mounted two projecting handholds. The angles of these, and the curves of the snath, allow a standing man to sweep the blade along just above the ground.

A cradle isn't often used any more; it's not needed and there are few left who have the skill and stamina to handle one. It was, essentially, a scythe with an added wooden frame above the blade. On this the cut grain fell, the straws lying neatly parallel; so the cradle gathered the grain as it cut it. Considering the added weight of the frame and that of the grain on top of it, it can be seen that a good man with a scythe wasn't necessarily good enough to stay with a cradle.

Once the crop was in the barn it could be threshed piecemeal on days when the weather didn't allow outside work, though it couldn't lie around too long or it would shatter and the mice would get it. Threshing was done by thumping the straw with hand flails until the kernels were knocked out of the heads onto the barn floor. The flail was simply a club, swiveled with leather at the end of a handle about six feet long.

After it was thoroughly beaten, and turned and beaten again, the straw was gathered up with a homemade wooden fork and stored to be used as animal bedding. What was left on the floor was a mixture of grain and chaff, which is the hulls and beards. This had to be swept up and winnowed, usually by hauling it up to the barn loft and pouring it onto a sheet spread below. By opening the doors on opposite sides of the barn a through draft was created that blew most of the light chaff out as the heavier grain fell. The chaff went down the necks and into the hair of everybody on the place. On still days big winnowing fans could be used, but only with backbreaking effort, so most people waited for a breeze.

Threshing with flails

Milling

Nothing could be more natural than for the Dutch to set up windmills to grind their grain to flour. The earliest known picture of New Amsterdam shows one of these. The general outward appearance of a windmill is familiar: a tower with four long arms. These arms are feathered a little and are made to revolve by the pressure of the wind blowing against the sails stretched on them. Modern mills in Holland and England have means of changing the angle of the feathering and automatic devices to keep the sails facing the wind. In earlier days the vanes were rigid and the necessary changes to adjust for wind direction had to be made by moving a long pole that had its upper end attached to the mill and its lower end reaching the ground. It was a common practice to equip the bottom of the pole with a wheel, to ease the job of moving it. This wheel wore a circular track all the way around the mill.

Two types of windmill were used in America, neither one exclusively anywhere. The more common mill was the "post" type. It was a box-like structure, set quite literally on a huge, heavily braced post. To get inside, it was usually necessary to climb a ladder and enter through a trap door in the floor. To head its sails into the wind, the whole structure was rotated on its post. The "smock" mill, which was the other kind, sat solidly on the ground and could be entered by a normal door. Its wheeled pole didn't move the whole building but only a mushroom-shaped cap.

A windmill's vanes turned a not-quite horizontal axle that in turn rotated a long vertical shaft by means of ingeniously made wooden gears. These made use of pegs as teeth and are more easily understood from a drawing than from description. The lower end of the long shaft turned the upper of two millstones. These were an enlargement of the hand quern that was described in the section about New England. The stones were usually called burrs. Some were chipped from a single block, but many of them were made up of segments carefully fitted and hooped together with heavy iron bands. The lower stone

72

was fixed and had grooves in its upper surface to promote grinding and to move the material across it. The two stones were enclosed and raw grain was dribbled to them through a hopper by hand. Later, an automatic jiggling regulator, known as a damsel, was invented. Various means were used to raise the grain to the top of the mill so that it could be run down on the burrs. The simplest was a drum hoist that hauled the bags up by a rope like the one illustrated. Later mills had elevators running in enclosed channels. Square channels carried belts with small buckets on them. Round ones had central shafts with wooden pegs set around them in a long spiral; these raised the loose grain as they rotated, using the principle discovered by Archimedes. All three kinds were powered by the sails.

After the grain was ground, it had still to be bolted by sifting it through meshes of increasing fineness. The coarser parts, the bran and middlings, could be fed to animals; the fine end product was, of course, flour, if the grain was wheat or rye. Wheat flour was bolted twice, being reground between boltings. Corn cannot readily be ground to the fineness of wheat flour.

A gristmill run by a water wheel wasn't different from one driven by sails, except that its power came from below and hence a different arrangement of the mechanism was necessary. Some explanation of the working of water wheels will be given further along in connection with the Southern sawmill. From Canada to Virginia both water mills and windmills ground grain and sawed wood.

New Amsterdam

For most of the seventeenth century the town on the tip of Manhattan Island was as completely Dutch as homesickness could make it, even to the ordering of a tidal inlet into the semblance of a short canal. With a cobbled lane on either side, the canal made a good place to land small boats and a bridge over it (not too far from the present Stock Exchange) was the favored trading spot for businessmen. The English filled in the canal and named it Broad Street. Traces of the Dutch village exist chiefly as place names now, such as Spuyten Duyvil, Coenties Slip, and The Bowery.

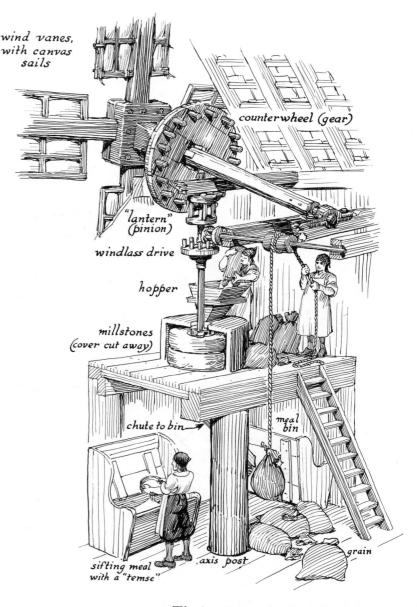

The interior mechanism of a windmill

Most of the larger houses followed the custom of Holland and had rather whimsical weather vanes on their roofs. The weather was a topic as interesting then as today. The rattle-watch on his rounds hourly disturbed the night by announcing time and weather. There was then no knob to turn that would shut him off, but his voice, echoing in the silent street, let his employers know he was still on the job. The rattle he carried was made just like the modern celebration noisemaker, in which a springy stick clatters on a toothed wheel, but it was larger and louder. It was used only to call for help in some emergency, like a fire. The streets the watch guarded weren't totally dark but they were nearly so. An ordinance required every seventh house to hang out a lantern on a pole during the dark of the moon. The houses between lanterns had to contribute candles.

Watchman's hourglass,
rattle, lantern, and mitten

Indian wampum

New Amsterdam was the trading center for the Colony. Shops did business on the ground floors of many houses. A lot of them were run by women. There was a scarcity of small change in America from its settlement until after it took over its own affairs. In New Netherland and in New England the need was filled for years by setting an arbitrary value on the Indians' bead wampum. The beads were laboriously made from quahaug shells and a higher value was put on those made from the purple part than on the white ones. It worked well until some smart white men started mass production of wampum with steel tools. The market was flooded and the value of the stuff vanished.

Goods never had fixed prices in the seventeenth century except when they were set by law, as in the case of bread. Even small purchases were made by bargaining; the shopkeeper asked more than he thought he could get, and the buyer offered less than he was willing to pay. Since both understood that, it all was a waste of time. The Quakers, settling wherever they could in the latter part of the century, brought with them conscience and common sense that required them to ask a fair price and stick to it. Quietly, they brought the rest of the world to their way of thinking.

Supplies for the back country, and furs, grain, and tobacco from the back country, were carried on the Hudson in little sloops or *vlie* boats. When the river froze, transportation stopped but communication was maintained by couriers who skated, all alone, through the great gorge. Of course, all Dutchmen could skate.

Dutch vlie *boat on the Hudson*

A courier to Fort Orange

An ancient patten skate.
The sharp pin was stuck into the shoe heel

People and Clothes

The people of New Netherland had a good time whenever they could. Sleighing and skating parties were frequent and kissing games enlivened indoor parties. The sport of coasting downhill on a sled was introduced by the Dutch, perhaps because hills were a novelty to them. A visiting lady from New England saw boys sledding in Albany and, after trying it out privately, gave it a low rating. What a pity no one could have recorded the experiment with a movie camera!

Weddings, christenings, and funerals were all times of social exuberance. Not only did the bride's father entertain at a wedding but, next day, the groom's father kept open house. Whenever it was necessary to collect money for a public project, or for the "church poor," the collectors waited for a wedding and made their touch when everybody was in good humor and a little gone in wine. This became an established custom. The bills for liquor and food for some of the funerals

show that a good time must have been had by all.

There were seldom any poor in the sense of economic misfits; any able-bodied person could make a living, but people became too old or too sick to work and they were cared for by the church. It was a Dutch custom to bind a bargain by dropping money in the poor box.

The Dutch were a religious people but most of them weren't stuffy about it. Attendance at church was expected but not compulsory. There were rules about Sunday behavior. Taverns weren't supposed to sell liquor during church hours; Sunday work, playing at bowls, and gaming were outlawed, and so was "drunken drinking."

Prosperity and a natural love for finery inclined the New Netherlanders to dress far more richly than the Puritans were able, or willing, to do. The Dutch followed the general style of the time with variations of their own. In an age of ballooning britches, a Dutchman's outswelled all others. His hat was a big plumed hat, not too well suited to his stocky build. Shoe buckles seem to have been popular with the Dutch before the other nations began to wear them. On the other hand, the prosperous among the Dutch clung to the starched ruff for some time after the English had abandoned it for the wide limp collar known as a "falling band." "Right out of the bandbox" originally meant nothing more than a clean collar.

Ruffs were a great nuisance and a great expense. They had to be laundered by experts. Some of the women who goffered them, when they were fashionable in London, made modest fortunes at it. The starched flutes, or goffers, were arranged on "setting sticks" and fixed into shape with hot, metal "poking sticks." Even then it was necessary to wear a wire "under-propper" to hold a ruff up. The starch used was frequently colored, perhaps because it showed dirt less easily. Blue and "goose

Collecting for the poor

green" were popular colors, so was yellow until a notorious murderess wore a yellow ruff to her execution.

Dutch women wore as many petticoats as did the Puritan women but they wore them striped and a lot shorter, to expose some length of dashingly clocked stocking. The fair New Netherlander wore a narrow girdle around her waist. Hanging from it, by ribbons or chains, was almost everything she might be likely to need: keys, scissors, pincushion, and a couple of embroidered pockets for extras. Instead of, or over, the bodice this lady often wore a loose, full-sleeved jacket. Covering her tightly pulled-back hair she wore a quilted cap, Irving says of calico, but in view of the rarity of cotton it was more likely made of printed linen. Much printing of linen was done in Holland.

Like the English youngsters, Dutch children were dressed as small adults, with the single difference that they wore wooden shoes. These were probably worn by farmers and workmen too, as they still are in the Netherlands. They are very practical in mud, if your feet can stand them. Children had a good time in New Netherland. They were loved and they weren't expected to behave like aldermen. Once in a while they got into some devilment and annoyed a minor functionary, who has left behind his plaintive report. There were few schools for some years and those that existed were plagued with a series of drunken schoolmasters. After the English took over they forbade the use of Dutch in schools. One teacher, who was himself Dutch (and no drunk), evolved a smart system for enforcing this. He issued a metal disk each day to the first boy who slipped into Dutch. The boys had the right to get rid of it by the same means, and he who held the token at the day's end was thrashed by the master. It happens that the Dutch word for "blunder" is *bok*. Can we have here the origin of the honored American custom of passing the buck?

The old Dutch custom of giving presents to children on December fifth, the Eve of *Sant Nikolaas,* when the saint was supposed to reward the good and turn the bad over for punishment to his servant, Black Ruprecht, became fused after 1664 with the English celebration of Christmas. Ruprecht vanished, but the jolly gentleman we know as Santa Claus is a neat blend of the gentle Saint and rollicking Father Christmas. Dr. Clement Moore, who wrote "A Visit From St. Nicholas" in New York, may have had something to do with the blending.

The now faded American custom of calling on all the neighbors on New Year's Day started in New Netherland. New Year's was a great holiday with them; so was May Day, when Maypoles were set up, and Shrovetide, when boisterous sports were in order, some of them involving regrettable cruelty to animals. Pinkster Day, at Whitsuntide, was a peculiarly Dutch celebration, a day for tricks and skylarking.

III. THE SOUTHERN COLONIES

Tobacco

The Virginians soon realized that gold mining would have to wait and, meanwhile, it was necessary to find some dull way to earn a living. John Rolfe, who also distinguished himself by marrying the Indian "princess," Pocahontas, solved the economic problem in 1612 by learning to cure tobacco that a white man could smoke. The Indian tobacco was bitter and rough. The Spanish had taught Europe to smoke by introducing the mild product of their South American colonies. The best "Oronooko" was the ideal and, from its name, Virginia and Maryland tobacco planters became known as "oronookoes." Rolfe's tobacco was good enough to find an immediate market in England, though not until 1655 did Virginia tobacco equal the Spanish in quality.

Everybody in Virginia dropped anything else he might be doing (which wasn't too much) and started planting tobacco. Carefully planned projects for silk-, glass-, and wine-making fell apart when the imported workmen chucked their jobs and went into the tobacco business. Tobacco was grown even in the streets of Jamestown. The weed itself became money. Clergymen and public officials were paid with it, so were taxes. When the famous shipload of "respectable maidens" was auctioned for matrimony at Jamestown in 1619, the cargo was paid for in tobacco. It was the chief, and almost the only, medium of exchange in both Virginia and Maryland until well into the eighteenth century. In large sections of both states it is still the major crop.

No written account of the early methods of

Hoeing tobacco

Sticking tobacco

"making" tobacco seems to have survived, possibly because they were jealously guarded secrets and were never written down. However, succeeding generations learned by doing, and the traditional ways that are still in use are probably not too different from those of the seventeenth century. The outline here describes the making of tobacco in southern Maryland today. Virginia does some things a little differently.

The dust-fine tobacco seed is sown, always on "new" ground, in woodland seedbeds, in January. In late May the seedling plants are set in rows in the field and are individually watered as they are planted. The two-foot-deep black loam, too rich for English wheat, that Colonial writers describe is gone now, destroyed by this same tobacco plant. Today the soil is used merely to hold the plants up; they grow on commercial fertilizer. In a proper patch, weeds are not allowed and their removal is mostly hoe work, as it was in the beginning.

Toward the end of July, when the sun is good and hot, flower buds form at the tops of the five-foot stalks and are removed by hand picking. Starting late in August, the still-green plants are cut off close to the ground and their butts are im-

Old tobacco barn

paled on slender sticks, five plants to a stick. A removable iron point is slipped on the stick to help it through the tough stems. The sticks hold the plants as they hang, head downward, in carefully ventilated barns to wilt and then cure until early winter.

When curing is complete the leaves are stripped off the stalks, "culled" (graded, that is), and carefully bunched in flat, fan-shaped "hands." These are stacked lying flat in meticulously made "burdens" about thirty inches high, for storage until the following summer. Then the tobacco is packed in hogsheads for shipment.

The hogsheads are homemade affairs, more drums than barrels. They are made of straight staves, not very closely fitted, and hooped with split saplings, just as has always been done. A hogshead is about five feet in diameter and as many feet long. Filling one is a thumping operation. With one wooden head in, it is first packed with as many "hands" as it will normally hold. Then it is placed in a horizontal screw press, called a "prize" in local language, and the contents of two casks, each of the same dimensions as the hogshead, are forced in on top of the original packing. A modern hogshead of tobacco, with both

Filling a tobacco hogshead with a "prize"

Signing an indenture in a ship's cabin

wooden ends in place, will weigh 750 to 800 pounds. In Colonial times they could squeeze only 500 pounds into one, and they usually called it a "cask" of tobacco.

It is customary in Virginia to pull the green leaves from the stalks in the field, and smoke is used as part of the curing process. An effort to find out if this was the method originated by Rolfe has met with no success.

Land and Bondage

Since the lower leaves of a tobacco plant are as much as two feet long, it's clear that raising the stuff needs plenty of land. When the boom started in Virginia, everybody grabbed all he could get. Any man who paid his own passage, or that of another, might have fifty acres. Land was granted in the names of sailors who scarcely set foot in the Colony and whose "head right" was sold to speculators by their skipper. To the violently expressed dismay of the Indians, the frontier was pushed quickly back to make room for plantations large and small. Some of the bigger ones ran up to 10,000 acres.

In addition to land, field hands were an absolute necessity and hard to come by. When the Dutch brought the first Negroes into Jamestown in 1619, they were snapped up immediately and put to work. They don't seem to have been consid-

ered slaves then, but merely servants whose passage money had been advanced by the plantation owners and who, like hundreds of whites who were brought in, were compelled to work without wages until the debt was paid. There were 300 Negro slaves in Virginia in 1649, but by then there were also Negroes who had discharged their debts and were free landowners. It wasn't until 1662 that Negroes were officially recognized as slaves, in bondage for life, whose children were born into the same condition, who could be bought and sold like cattle, and whose families could be broken up at the will of an owner. Nearly everybody in the seventeenth century thought of slavery as perfectly normal. Slaves came to be owned in all the Colonies; even the Quakers held slaves, though with increasing qualms of conscience. The New Englanders made a pious law against slavery, with careful loopholes left in it; they couldn't own a slave unless he was a war captive—or unless someone offered a slave for sale!

Thousands of white men and women who came penniless into this country and had to serve a term at labor were known as indentured servants, bondservants, or redemptioners. They came to all the Colonies, clear up to the Revolutionary War and even after it. Most of them came to the South, because there was more need for them there. Whether they came willingly or not, they signed (or marked) an agreement to work a stated num-

*Bondsman wearing
a "pot hook" iron collar*

ber of years, usually four or five. The "owner" paid the equivalent of a couple of hundred dollars for the servant's passage, agreed to feed and clothe him for the term of service and, at its end, to provide certain items to help with a new start in the world.

The nature of these terminal gifts varied from place to place and from contract to contract. Usually they included a suit of clothes, a hoe, and an ax. Sometimes the servant also received a barrel of corn and, if he was smart enough to have it properly set forth in his indenture, fifty or a hundred acres of land. As bait, the standard form of contract read "land according to the custom of the country," but the custom of the country in the South awarded the land to the plantation owner, not to the servant. Warnings against this double talk were published in London, but they were wasted; too few could read them.

Even those who were given land were likely to pass it up and head for the frontier, where they could set up in business on far more than fifty acres, regardless of the fact that it belonged officially to some lord in England. The descendants of a good many of these squatters are still on the land their ancestors appropriated. England was far away.

White bond-servants were as completely slaves, during their term of service, as were Negroes. They could be compelled to work at anything, for any number of hours a day, and they could be whipped at the will of the master. For this reason, as well as to avoid their debts, many of them ran away and numbers of them were never caught, since there was nothing to distinguish them from any other colonist. Recaptured runaways sometimes had an iron collar, called a "pot hook," welded around their necks. Life wasn't as hard for white servants in the early days, when their labor was essential to the existence of the Colonies, as it became later, when slaves were plentiful. And always, anyone who understood the "mystery" of a trade or craft, or who had enough education to act as a clerk or a teacher, could be sure of good treatment. Women were usually assigned as house servants but the rougher ones (and some were as rough as is possible) were sent to the fields with a hoe.

Men who were able to pay their own passage and expected to buy land sometimes bound themselves out as servants for experience and a chance to look about them. Incidentally, such solvent persons were advised to bring a bed with them, if they would have any hope of finding lodgings. Some, who had no money, came willingly for a new start in life, but by far the majority of indentured servants were brought over forcibly. More than half of these were "trepanned" (kidnaped) in English seacoast towns, but many were "transported" as legal punishment.

Laws in England were harsh, and decent judges were often glad of an opportunity to sentence a man to service in the Colonies, rather than hang him for stealing a shilling. So, hundreds of redemptioners had records of crime, but the conditions that made them criminals in England didn't exist in America and a fair percentage of them prospered and begat descendants of distinguished value to the country. On the other hand, some of them were no good to start with and worsened. It was never considered disgraceful to have been an indentured servant, which is just as well, since most of our ancestors got their starts that way.

Small Planters

When a bond-servant had worked out his time, he might have to continue for a while as a paid laborer in order to be able to buy the basic needs of setting up for himself. Often, however, a decent master would have allowed him to cultivate a

A freed bondsman looking over his new plantation

indentured servant, who, on a small place, wou[ld] live as a member of the family; then he would g[et] *two* servants and perhaps a slave or two; and [fi]nally he would get more land.

He was a poor husbandman. In his haste to raise tobacco he planted little else and found himself with a big crop of "sotweed" and nothing to eat; nor could he readily trade his tobacco for food, because his neighbors had done the same thing. No fertilizer was used and the lone crop exhausted even the virgin land quickly. The thing to do then was to move farther back and clear more land, abandoning the old place to scrub pine. When this move was made, it was customary to burn down one's house in order to recover the nails from it. To prevent this, the Virginia Colony offered any migrant an equivalent quantity of nails if he would leave his house intact.

Cottages

The first dwelling of a small planter was probably a hut with a catted clay chimney. In time one-room frame cottages were built. They had steep thatched roofs and were framed of hewn timbers, exactly the way the New England houses were built and, like them, had their outside walls covered with riven clapboards, only Southerners called them weatherboards and still do. A few houses had saltbox roofs, but in Virginia they were "catslide" roofs. The chief difference from the early Northern house was in the chimney, and in

small plot while he was still in service, from which he might make enough to buy the tools, the nails, the salt, the gunpowder, that were indispensable.

The land he bought, was given, or took usually lay in the back country and was wooded with primeval forest. The bayside and river-fronting land was grabbed by the large plantations.

As soon as he had put up some kind of shelter for himself, the new "oronooko's" task was to clear enough land for a first crop. For a man alone, with only an ax, to fell and cut up the huge oaks, hickories, and chestnuts, many of them five or six feet thick, would have been impossible. What he did was to girdle the trees, as the Pilgrims did for planting their corn, and let them stand where they were until they were quite dead and dried out; then he set fire to them. Thousands of acres of American land were cleared that way. The new settler might make shift to raise his first small crop among the trees before they had dried enough to burn. Even after they were down he had stump trouble for years. The stumps of such trees were not casually to be pulled, and there was no dynamite.

As he prospered, and prosper a good many did, especially in the early years when tobacco was still five shillings a pound, our planter would aspire to a wife, who would cook for him and help him in the fields, and to an ox, or a span of oxen, to help with the heavy work; then he would yearn for an

The frame cottage of a small tobacco planter

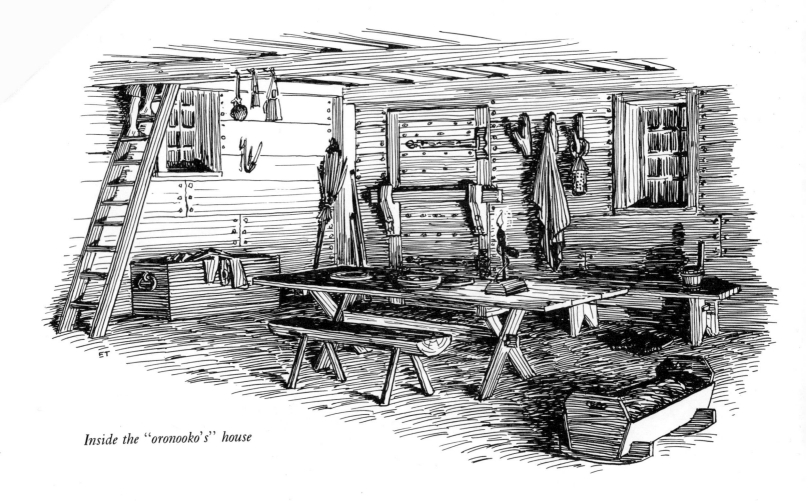

Inside the "oronooko's" house

the absence of that vestibule called a porch. Southern houses usually had their fireplaces built outside the walls, against one end, and of course accessible from inside. The upper part of the chimney stood a foot or more clear of the building, as a precaution against fire. Chimneys were built of brick and were so large that the base was sometimes as wide as the house. Stone was scarce, so brick was made very early; in Virginia the first bricks were burnt in 1611.

Windows were small and usually shuttered for protection, not only from the Indians but also from the summer heat. It's improbable that many small houses had glass windows; oiled paper or horn scraped thin were used as substitutes. It wasn't possible to see through either substance but they let in a little light. When glass could be had, it was set in lead frames, or calmes.

The lone room of a house like this was about twenty feet square. The floor, if it wasn't of packed earth, was likely to be brick, not set in mortar but laid dry on a couple of inches of sand. The front door was made of heavy hewn planks, often of two thicknesses. The walls were covered with pit-sawn

sheathing, the boards being more often horizontal than was usual in the North; often, too, they were whitewashed. One whole wall was taken up by the fireplace, in which logs eight feet long could be burned and at one side of which was a brick oven, such as has been described. Cooking methods and utensils were the same as those used in the North and the food itself was similar, except for the regional differences in game and fish.

Of the interior furnishings of such a house little can be said with assurance. Most of the owners were too poor to have brought much furniture with them, or to import any in their earlier years in this country. There wasn't the habit of home craftsmanship that prevailed in New England. These facts seem to leave a pretty bare room, with perhaps a plain chest, some "forms" or benches, made of halves of split logs with peg legs, a "sawbuck" table of hewn planks, and a bedstead that was merely a frame with, perhaps, strips of rawhide across it to support the bedding. At worst there was no bed at all, but a pile of straw on the floor; that is all an ordinary offered the poorer sort of traveler.

Ways and Means

The best eyewitness description of an oronooko and his way of life is given by Ebenezer Cook in his "epic," *The Sot-Weed Factor;* it doesn't make either very attractive. However, Ebenezer tried to make a quick profit in tobacco and was soured when he lost his money by being too trusting. So his description needs to be salted a little. Cook's Maryland planter was a boor, living in squalor, with hospitality as his only virtue. This was frontier country then, and no doubt manners were rough and speech blunt, as they always have been on all frontiers. Certain it is that the Southern Colonies had bad reputations in England. Past the middle of the century, men who had been over here were still publishing pamphlets to try to overcome the prejudice.

After the second Indian massacre in Virginia, in 1623, it was realized that man cannot live by tobacco alone and some attention was given to planting corn, flax, and fruit. Cattle and hogs ran wild in the woods, the cattle earmarked with various notchings that denoted their owners and that were duly entered in the local parish records.

All tobacco was shipped by water. In order to get theirs to market, the smaller planters usually had to load it at the wharf of a large plantation. The casks had to be rolled overland to the wharf, since few of the little fellows were located on the water. The trails made by this operation were the "rolling roads," the first roads in the South. Sometimes the casks were pushed by manpower but, for longer distances (some rolling roads are twenty miles long), an axle was thrust all the way through the cask, its ends supporting a timber frame to which a span of oxen could be hitched.

The great size of the tobacco plantations scattered the populations of Virginia and Maryland. Instead of farms clustered about small towns, as in the North, every plantation became a sort of town in itself. The two Colonies had one principal center each—Jamestown and St. Mary's. Even when county seats were created they scarcely deserved to be called towns for many years. Besides the courthouse, the "gaol," and the church, there might be an ordinary, a smithy, and perhaps a struggling store.

Not *everybody* raised tobacco. Some found another way to make a fast shilling. Late in the seventeenth century when England tried to grab *all* the profits from her colonies, regardless of their welfare, by restricting their imports to her products, the colonists started smuggling. It was done up and down the whole coast, and nowhere was a smuggler harder to catch than along the lonely beaches of Virginia and Maryland. Many a tax-free bolt of silk and cask of brandy came in through the breakers; and many a cask of tobacco went out through them, to fetch a better price in Holland than London would pay. Hidden trading posts were operated where transactions were carried on through a small window, with buyer and seller theoretically invisible to each other. On the Eastern Shore of Maryland there is today a hamlet named Hole-in-the-wall.

The Big Plantations

Each of the important plantations had its own wharf where ships picked up its tobacco and at which the same vessels landed the purchases of the planter and his family, ordered through the plant-

Rolling tobacco

A plantation wharf

er's agent or "factor" in London: the furniture, the "plate" (silver), the doublets and shoes that never fitted, the petticoats that were always the wrong color. These enormous farms supplied almost nothing to the Colony and bought practically nothing in it. The system was not only bad for the Colony, it was bad for the planter too. In nearly every case, he was deeply and permanently in debt.

The price of tobacco fluctuated and overplanting often brought it so low that it was worthless. The planter went on buying just the same. He was completely at the mercy of his factor—the price of tobacco was what the factor said he could get for it. The prices of goods bought in London were doubled and redoubled by the time the goods were delivered at the planter's wharf. Distance made it difficult to settle accounts properly; debts passed from father to son along with the land. Some families stayed in debt for 150 years. However, the lordly living associated with Southern planters belonged to the eighteenth century. In the seventeenth it was simple to the point of crudity until after 1650, and far from luxurious even then.

The Manor Houses

The owners of the larger plantations lived in brick houses—not brick mansions, just houses. Several are standing; one of them, in Princess Anne County, Virginia, built by Adam Thoroughgood, who came over as an indentured servant and became a man of substance, is probably the oldest house in the eastern United States. By eliminating the changes that later owners are known to have made, it is possible to get from this house a fair idea of the home of a prosperous, or anyway notably indebted, seventeenth-century planter. Such a man had the same national origin that the Puritans had, but his way of life and his climate were different, so his house came out different also.

The temperature in Virginia dropped below freezing now and then but not often far below and it didn't stay there long, so there was no need to conserve heat by building a house around a chimney stack. The larger houses had their chimneys at the ends, just as the little frame houses had, and like them built the stack part standing a little away from the wall. Most of these houses had two rooms downstairs and two sleeping rooms under the roof. The big chimneys were narrowed above the first floor to accommodate small fireplaces in the attic, then narrowed above that for the flues.

Because miles of their hunting forest was rapidly destroyed for tobacco land, and because of stupid white arrogance, the Indians in Virginia actively resented the English invasion earlier than the Indians did elsewhere. The settlers had good reason to be afraid of them, so the first plantation houses had loopholes for firing guns from the upper rooms and "hideyholes" next to the fireplaces, between the walls. Sometimes there were underground passages leading from the hiding places to the water's edge, to provide a way of escape. The Thoroughgood house had all of these things.

*The "Big House" of a large plantation.
Based upon the Adam Thoroughgood house*

The windows of the old houses have sliding wooden sash in them now. Originally they were divided into four sections, like those of the Dutch houses in New Netherland, with leaded casements in the lower two sections and immovable leaded sash in the upper ones. Above each window and over the plank door was a low arch of brick. Of nearly every old brick house in eastern America it has been said at some time that "the bricks were brought over from England." Occasionally a ship loaded with a lightweight cargo needed ballast in her hold to keep her down in the water so she'd "handle" properly; bricks would serve for this and some *are* known to have been brought over in that way, but only a very few.

Bricks

There was plenty of clay in America and thousands of bricks used for Colonial buildings were made here by hand. A kiln was set up near a clay bank where there was also plenty of firewood and ample water. The freshly dug clay was first thrown into a hole and "wet down" for a week by pouring water over it. Then it was shoveled into a pugmill and still more water was put in with it. The pugmill mixed and "worked" the clay and water into a smooth, plastic consistency. Most Colonial pugmills used ox-power. Plodding in a circle that he learned to follow without human supervision, the ox towed one end of a long pole that provided plenty of leverage to rotate the vertical shaft of the mill. The shaft revolved in the middle of a wooden box and was itself nothing more than a wooden post. Projecting horizontally from the first three feet or so of the shaft's lower end a number of iron pins were arranged in a descending spiral. The pins were spaced so that they could cut through the clay, yet at the same time they forced it steadily downward and slowly squeezed it out of a small hole at the bottom of the box.

Near the outlet the mold man worked, standing in a waist-deep pit so that he wouldn't have to stoop to pick up clay. He would take up a lump, roll it in sand, and press it into a wooden mold that had itself been dipped in sand while wet. The

Mixing brick clay in a pugmill. The molder is in his pit and a wooden brick mold lies in the foreground

purpose of the sand was to keep the bricks free in the mold so they would readily slide out. Molds had spaces for from four to eight bricks. When the mold was completely filled, the top surface was scraped smooth and the shaped clay was dumped onto a board to dry in the air for two or three weeks.

Colonial bricks were baked with the heat of wood fires, kept burning continuously for ten days. The "green" bricks were stacked in walled kilns so as to form long tunnels, connecting at both ends with openings in the base of the kiln walls. The

bricks were stacked with their ends, or "headers," facing the tunnel, and spaces were left between bricks so the heat could circulate through the stack.

The fire burned in the tunnels. Wood was stoked through the holes in the outside wall. There were really half a dozen fires in the kiln, one in each tunnel. In the South, hard oak was burned and it made so hot a fire that the headers nearest the flame were actually vitrified into coarse glass; perhaps it was the sand that glazed. Anyway, it produced a bluish shiny surface on one end of all the bricks lining the tunnels. This made a novel and handsome effect, a mingling of pink and blue, dull and shiny, when laid in the Flemish bond. By laying the bricks alternately lengthwise and endwise, this system forms a checkered pattern in a wall.

The Southerners didn't have to resort to mud for mortar. Chesapeake Bay supplied any quantity of oyster shells that could be burnt into lime and mixed with sand. Mounds of shells, accumulated for generations by the Indians, were found along the shores. Oyster-shell lime was also used for plastering and whitewashing inside walls.

A close view of bricks with glazed headers, laid in Flemish bond

86

After the middle of the century a few larger houses were built. They looked so impressive that people called them "castles"! A famous one is still standing: "Bacon's Castle," built in Surrey County, Virginia, in the style of an Elizabethan manor house long after that style had gone out of fashion. It was a cross-shaped house and, though it had only the usual two rooms on the first floor, there was a vestibule, making one arm of the cross, and a rear stair-tower making another. This house had a full second floor with bedrooms, and more of them over that in the attic.

"Bacon's Castle"

Furniture

The furniture in these houses was simple; some was homemade but not nearly so much of it as in Puritan houses. The planters had other interests and they didn't have as much furniture-making weather to confine them indoors as the Northerners had. The plantation houses started with the same kind of long tables, joint stools, and wainscot chairs that the Yankees used, but they imported nearly all of them from England. Before the century was out they were buying furniture from Massachusetts. Ships from Boston and Salem brought not only wooden articles but also wicker chairs and tin candlesticks. Sugar and salt came in the same cargo. As payment the skippers preferred pork, rather than tobacco or furs. Hard money they couldn't hope to get.

After 1650 tobacco prosperity began to create a certain amount of luxury. Comparatively light "banister-back" armchairs were new in England and were sent over by factors. They were also made in New England. The banister back itself was made of turned spindles that had been split in half lengthwise, to present a flat surface instead of a knobby one to the human spine. Space-saving gate-leg tables, called "flap tables," appeared, and "Turkey-work" (Oriental) carpets were used to

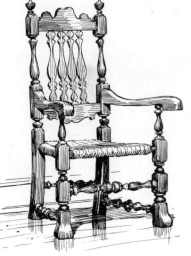

A banister-back chair of the sort made in New England and sold in the South

A "flap" table. Made without the use of a lathe. Such a table might be the work of a clever slave

A bed with plain linen curtains, or "bed furniture"

A Southern kitchen

cover them. A carpet on a floor would have seemed odd in the seventeenth century. Rugs, too, weren't for the floor; they were bedcovers and they were made like bedcovers, not like what we think of as a rug. Beds were the curtained four-poster kind that could provide a little privacy in a house that had no hallways.

Cooking

The warm climate and an ample supply of servants combined to suggest to the Southern planter that his cooking be done outside the house. A separate kitchen building was put up near one end of the residence and from it food was rushed in, often in covered dishes. In winter it could be kept warm or reheated on the hearth in the hall. Even in early days a few houses had passageways between house and kitchen. "Bacon's Castle" had one, so had some Maryland houses. The kitchen building looked like the cottage of a minor planter and often it actually was. When a larger house was built, the old one was left standing and demoted.

One whole wall of the kitchen was filled by a fireplace where the cooking utensils and methods were exactly the same as those used in the poorest houses, and as those in all the other Colonies. One

advantage it had: a swinging iron crane, from which pots could be hung, without all the nuisance of lug poles and trammels, was used in the South from very early times.

Food

As it was elsewhere, corn was the mainstay of diet, and even the most dedicated tobacco grower learned perforce to raise enough of it to provide for the needs of his family and "hands." He even made beer of it. The Bay and the salt "rivers" yielded unlimited fish, oysters, and crabs. Terrapins, which are water turtles that don't stay in the water, are now considered a rare delicacy; once they were so common that a humanitarian Maryland law forbade their being fed to slaves more than three times a week.

Waterfowl were as plentiful as fish, and the planter who could afford a wheel-lock gun that could be wound up in advance and held ready to shoot could easily get the best that the world provides for his table. The cheaper guns of the time, the kind that were sometimes given to bond-servants when their terms were finished, were match-locks. These weren't very good for hunting because the game usually departed before the smoldering match could be adjusted to fire the priming. A light crossbow could be set in advance, like a wheel lock, and used for stalking birds and small game. That such bows were used was proved recently, when Mr. Louis Caywood of the National Park Service found a "goat's foot" near Jamestown. This was an ingenious iron lever for setting a crossbow.

Pigs and an occasional beef could be killed on a large place and consumed immediately. This was desirable even in winter, because the weather wasn't consistently cold enough to allow fresh meat to be kept safely. A small planter shared a kill with the neighbors, expecting and getting a return of the favor in due time. Meat was salted and smoked to preserve it, and it was also possible to keep meat by cooking it, putting it, hot, into a crock, and covering it with a deep layer of melted fat. This was often done for breaking the diet monotony on sea voyages and was a fairly successful method of preservation, though nobody knew why it was, or why it sometimes failed. There's no question that Colonial stomachs were stronger than modern ones; meat had to be in really bad shape before it was considered uneatable. The strong sage flavor that is still given to fresh sausage was originally introduced for a practical purpose.

Most of the wealthy planters were hearty fellows, and they founded a tradition of good eating. It was the custom in England at the time to load the table with food, particularly on special occasions; the same thing was done in Virginia and Maryland. Fish, crabs, oysters, game, and several meats, with a long list of vegetables, and with hot bread, all at the same meal, were quite usual. After all, there were plenty of mouths to eat the leftovers. This custom of an excessive plenty was continued and some remnants of it still exist.

The hours for meals weren't the same in Colonial times as they are now. Our planter rose early, drank his morning beer, and went off with his overseer to inspect the crops. About ten o'clock he brought an imposing appetite back to the house for breakfast. The main dish for this meal might be beef, or a turkey. Hens hadn't then had the training in production they received later, so eggs were not yet a universal breakfast dish. If one accumulated enough to serve, "a dish of eggs" made a tidbit for a party.

After breakfast the planter attended to business,

A planter and his overseer on morning inspection

or family matters, until dinnertime, which was three thirty or four in the afternoon. After dinner, more business, or social visiting, with supper at about nine at night and bed soon after, though special suppers have been known to last most of the night. The time between dinner and supper was called the "evening," and Southerners still confuse strangers when they say evening and mean late afternoon.

Lumber and Sawmills

The planter's kitchen was only the first of many small structures that gradually gathered around the "Big House." In addition to stable, storehouse, and smokehouse, the plantation needed a carpenter shop, a blacksmith shop, a cobbler's shop, and living quarters for the slaves and servants who worked in them. Spinning house, weaving house, and schoolhouse were later additions. The tobacco barns and the field-slave quarters were some distance from the main group of buildings.

The outbuildings were usually of frame construction and many planks were required to build them. Hand sawing was done at first, but most large plantations eventually had water-powered sawmills to meet the need. Labor was available but it was more profitably used in the tobacco field than in the saw-pit. Even in the very flat country east of the Bay it was usually possible to dam a stream and get fall enough to turn a water wheel; if not, there was always the wind.

Until the beginning of the nineteenth century a sawmill was nothing more than a mechanical way to work a pit saw. It operated very slowly but it could make two or more cuts at the same time, which hand sawing couldn't accomplish, and the work required only a minimum of human muscle and time. It may be assumed that all Southern mills had overshot wheels. For these no great "fall" is needed; it's necessary only to have a sufficient *volume* of water, high enough above the wheel to pour onto its upper surface.

A mill with a wheel of this kind had to be built well downstream from the dam that formed its millpond. Water was brought to the wheel by a ditch or millrace that followed a more nearly level course than did the parent stream. When it reached the mill the water in the race was flowing sluggishly, as much as twelve or fifteen feet above the stream bed. At the lower end of the millrace the water passed through a gate that controlled its flow into a trough, leading it just past the top center of the mill wheel, where it poured out into the wheel's buckets. The buckets were so shaped that they dumped their water at the bottom of the wheel, thus keeping the wheel out of balance and causing it to turn.

Some minor liberties have been taken in making the accompanying illustration. There seemed to be no other way to get all of the parts into one drawing. Naturally the mill would be capable of cutting a much longer timber. The water wheel is too small by half for the rest of the mechanism, and it would ordinarily be considerably lower than the crank bearings.

Overshot wheels came in varying diameters and widths. A small water supply with considerable fall could make the best use of a large, narrow wheel; a big volume of water with little fall could

90

reach only a wheel of small diameter, so the wheel was made wide, to carry as great a weight of water in each bucket as possible. Weight on the wheel was power, and power not speed was the object. Ten revolutions a minute was fair speed for a mill wheel; for grinding grain this was increased by gearing, but for sawmills it was geared still slower. In a sawmill, the shaft of the large gear, that received power from a pinion on the water-wheel shaft, turned a crank with a throw long enough to move the saws their full length. The saws were set side by side in a rectangular sash. A simple connecting rod, the pitman, joined the crank and the bottom of the sash and moved the sash up and down in two greased grooves. It was necessary to press the work steadily against the saw blades in order to make a continuous cut. In primitive mills this was done by the pull of a couple of weights hung on ropes. The ropes passed over a roller and were attached to the downstream end of the sliding carrier that supported the saw log. Better mills had a ratchet, taking power from the mill wheel, that advanced the carrier about half an inch with each cut.

All wasn't pie for the sawyer. At the end of a cut the mill was stopped by closing the sluice gate, and the sawn planks were removed and piled. Then the heavy carriage had to be dragged back along its track and a new timber jimmied into place for the next cut. Of course, once a cut was started, the sawyer could go on about other business. There was a stop on the timber carrier and, when the cut reached its full length, the saw would just move up and down in the air until somebody turned off the water.

Plantation People

Clothing the number of people required to work a large tobacco plantation was a difficult problem. Some planters imported cheap cloth and cut and sewed it with slave labor. But it proved cheaper to raise flax and spin and weave it on the place, again with slave labor. The universal clothing in the tobacco field was made of blue linen. Since there were almost no sheep in the South during the seventeenth century, all wool cloth had to be imported. Some of it came from Puritan looms, in spite of the objections of English cloth workers.

The isolated group posed other problems, too.

Building a coffin by candlelight

When hands "took sick" they were doctored by the planter's wife to the best of her ability, with about as good results as could have been obtained any other way. Doctors were so scarce as to be practically nonexistent and weren't held in very high esteem anyway. The opinion was expressed in Virginia that the Indian medicine men were as good as any European doctor, and there was probably truth in it.

Death struck all ages and all classes with impartial frequency. The most dangerous time was infancy. The majority of people who survived to the age of fifty were married at least twice, and it wasn't at all unusual for a person of either sex to acquire five mates in a lifetime. It would be interesting to know how some few *did* manage to survive to real old age. The dead were buried, without delay, in wooden coffins of a shape that conformed, roughly, to the human body. These were built to measure by the local carpenter, and their production was no small part of his business.

Dentistry didn't exist at this time. No one dreamed that anything could be done to halt the decay of a tooth; it just decayed until it hurt too badly to endure and then the strongest man on the place pulled it out. Barbers often did a little tooth-pulling, but it was more often the chore of the local blacksmith. The result, of course, was that even young people and the most elegant of adults showed gaps when they smiled. Many a person was completely toothless at thirty.

A gentleman's spice cabinet

Accurate figures on how much liquor was consumed per colonist are hard to come by, but it's easy to gather that practically all men and a great many women started drinking before breakfast and kept at it pretty steadily until bedtime. Hard cider replaced English beer in the North, but apples were scarcer around the Chesapeake, so the planters made shift to brew beer from corn. Nearly every cottage had its big brew-kettle in a corner. They also did some distilling of stronger stuff. Wine, rum, brandy, and, at the end of the century, gin were imported in great quantities. In the South rum was considered plebeian, to be drunk by the populace on holidays, but not by gentlemen—unless of course there was nothing else to drink.

Mixed drinks were as popular then as now but they were entirely different. Few of them were so powerful as the modern cocktail, ounce for ounce, but they were drunk from larger bumpers. The very thought of some of the combinations makes a modern stomach shudder. Almost any kind of distilled or fermented liquor was casually stirred into beer. Milk, dry white wine, and spice made sack posset. Hot spiced wine with an egg in it made flip. Many drinks were spiced, so a gentleman usually had his own spice cabinet near the fireplace in the hall. It's possible that the mere costliness of spices made them seem a desirable addition to a potation. Frequently a pot of beer, or a noggin of spiced wine, was mulled (that is, heated)

by sticking a red-hot poker into it. The resulting flavor usually fails to charm the modern palate.

The casual hospitality of the plantation houses, where great and mean were always welcome and no limit was set on the length of the visits, isn't merely a romantic story. Isolated as he was, and by nature gregarious, the planter was hungry for company and for *news.* There were no newspapers. He could find out what was going on in the world and in the Colony only by letters and by word of mouth. So, if a strange boat beat up the river, it was hailed ashore and its passengers were invited up to the house. If a road ran near his place, the planter was quite likely to keep a slave posted at the entrance to his mile-long lane to invite *all* travelers to come in and rest a spell. The custom was so universal that innkeepers bitterly complained that it hurt their business.

Mostly there was no road. Visits from one plantation to another were made by water and the habit was maintained long after roads were built, because it was often quicker to get where you were going by boat. The shores of the Chesapeake are so laced by twisting waterways that one's neighbor across the creek may live twenty miles away by road.

The mistress on a large plantation had little or no laborious work to do but, in addition to a kind of maternal interest in everybody on the place, she had the responsibility of all the servants and slaves connected with the Big House. Most of these were women, of course. She supervised such things as cookery, laundry, meat preservation, and the drying of fruits and vegetables. If there was spinning and weaving on the place, it was done under her eye. She herself and her older daughters might work with the sewing women, closely watching them and helping them.

No doubt Mistress Oronooko had her regular rounds of inspection, as her husband had. If she wasn't a "lady" originally, she came to think of herself as one and she handed down a tradition that a lady does not do menial work. She was likely to be on friendly, almost intimate terms with the Negro house slaves, and they quite freely "talked back" to her as long as they didn't forget that subtle subservience known as their "place."

Twice a year everybody who could do it went to the principal town to do public and private business and to have a good time. Trades were made,

Punishing a scold on the ducking stool

slaves and servants were bought and sold, and some notable games of chance were played. Drinking mounted in a great crescendo. The Assemblies met (they were the grandsires of Congress); they argued with the Governor; the younger people flirted, and danced, and showed off their clothes. The courts sat; and if anyone needed hanging he was hanged and everybody turned out to see the show.

A person accused of a really serious crime, even murder, could still get off *one time* if he could plead benefit of clergy. That is, if he proved in open court that he could read, he was branded with a "T" on the brawn, or fleshy part, of the left thumb —and released. The brand kept him from ever repeating. This privilege (and what a privilege!) was generally allowed in the Colonies. It was left over from the time when readers were scarce and valuable.

There wasn't so much minor day-to-day punishment in the South as in New England. Still, it wasn't too unusual for a bad-tempered woman to be cooled down by a good drenching on the ducking stool. This instrument of "torture" was made like a well sweep extending over a creek or a pond. The victim was tied on the long end. Strong men handled the short end and soused her repeatedly in the water. This was far more terrible punishment to a seventeenth-century damsel, who would never have dreamed of going into the water voluntarily, than it may seem in this day of universal swimming. Certain masculine offenders in all the Colonies were sentenced to be "whipped at the tail

of a cart." This meant they were compelled to walk behind a cart to which their hands were tied, while one, who followed the culprit, whipped him at every step, all through the town.

The town, in the case of Jamestown, was a compact replica of an English village. St. Mary's, where nobody was ever much afraid of Indians, seems to have spread out more, and its houses, though just as English, weren't so strictly town houses. The foundations dug up at Jamestown show clearly that the houses faced the street, "in two faire rows," with no yards in front of them and no space between them. No picture of these buildings is known. The representation of them, in the background of the next illustration, is based on English town houses of the time.

Clothes

Even in the early days of Jamestown, the Virginians seem to have had a tendency to be dressy. We read a scathing comment on a cowkeeper who went "in flamynge silk" and an ex-collier's wife who wore a "fair perle hatband." In 1610 Lord Delaware attended church there with a guard of fifty liveried halberdiers and, no doubt, clad himself to shame the sun. The habit of fine clothes didn't abate with time, as is attested by surviving lists of goods ordered from London. However, dressing up seems to have been for company and for visits to town; complaints exist of the sloppy dress of even the most important planters when they were at home.

Jamestown, about 1670.
The Governor and his lady wear the latest thing from London

The cycle of style in the South followed that of England more closely than it was followed up around Boston, because of inclination, credit, and closer contact with the source. If a newly arrived governor turned out in the latest Charles II tunic, then every rich planter up the James, or up the Patuxent, must have one like it, as soon as sail could fetch it.

The late seventeenth century was a time of radical change in men's clothes. They went through a very fancy phase in England, just after Charles II was restored to the throne, but the style was too short-lived to have much effect in America, and it was almost unnoticed in New England. However, an account survives of a dandified British sea captain who appeared there in a "jackanapes" suit, with "Rhinegrave" breeches, looped all over with ribbons. He swaggered through Boston and was annoyed by a crowd of hooting boys.

A suggestion made to King Charles by the diarist John Evelyn resulted in the beginnings of the coat as we know it. It was a knee-length, straight-up-and-down tunic, imitating the clothes of the Persians. Visiting Englishmen wore them here, and tunics, or "vests" as they were called, were imported by wealthy Americans. By 1680 the skirts of the tunics spread and they became coats; then they began to be worn in America by ordinary men, as well as by dandies.

With the coat came the wig, one of the weirdest fashions that man has indulged in. At first it was a periwig, "full-bottomed," falling over the shoulders in carefully arranged ringlets, kept in order at prodigious expense, and made to look like the kind of human hair that most heads couldn't grow. The imitation of nature was soon forgotten. Periwigs were tried that were shoulder-length on the right side and breast-length on the left. These were fol-

94

lowed in time by all sorts of shapes, colors, and materials, none of which made any pretense of being the wearer's own hair. They were wigs, and they were worn as garments.

Women's fashions didn't change so violently as did men's. Their hair went up in short curls or down in long ones; various indoor head-coverings were added, or subtracted; the neck was bared or covered in different ways; the overskirt was looped up this way or that way; but the basic bodice and full skirt remained unchanged for a long time. At times, fashionable ladies extended their petticoats on frameworks of various kinds. There *were* fashionable ladies in America quite early, even in New England. The wife of one of the Massachu-

setts governors, living on a farm, on the edge of wilderness, made a great pother over importing the latest London fancies. She was exceptional in the North; she would not have been in the South.

Southern women wore basically the same clothes their Northern sisters wore, but with no restraint on such things as huge "virago" sleeves, lace collars, and elaborate embroidery. They wore a frizz of "bull's head" curls across their foreheads, and went masked in public. The total effect would have been conspicuous in Boston. Southern children wore petticoats, pinners, and hanging sleeves, like Puritan children; but the petticoat was likely to be velvet, yes, velvet, the pinner, silk, and the sleeves, enriched with needlework.

Coats in the time of William and Mary.
The man on the left still clings to a James II style.
The lady wears a high frontage

No one worried too much about personal cleanliness. Keeping one's body and clothes always clean was an idea that first occurred to Beau Brummell, in the nineteenth century. Not that no bathing was done. There is evidence that the more elegant took a day off about once a month to "make themselves clean." The process was seriously thought to entail some risk. Yet some ladies took what they believed was elaborate care of their complexions, rising before dawn and collecting the dew from the grass to apply to their faces. If this and all else failed, an ornamental black patch, shaped like a circle or star or crescent, was used to cover a pimple.

Learning

The first Southern college, William and Mary, was not founded until 1693. Not very many seventeenth-century Southerners were interested in culture, and headquarters was willing to keep things that way. Governor Berkeley of Virginia wrote in 1671, "I thank God there are no free schools or printing . . . for learning has brought disobedience and heresy and sects into the world and printing has divulged them, and libels against the government." The sons of wealthy planters were sent to England to be educated; their daughters got along in contented illiteracy, as did most of the common folk of both sexes.

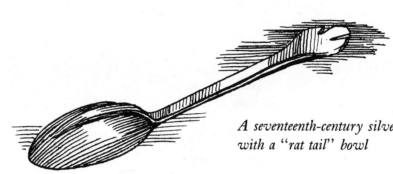

A seventeenth-century silver spoon with a "rat tail" bowl

The Eighteenth Century

Wooden horse rake

Town crier

*Windvane from a mill
in which William Penn was a partner*

I. PENNSYLVANIA

Philadelphia

The seventeenth century had nearly twenty years to run when the first Quaker colonists dug themselves caves in the river bank where Philadelphia was to be, but these were the advance guard of a new century. As the town grew it was laid out in neat rectangular blocks according to plan and, right from the start, its houses had the tidy look that belongs to the eighteenth century. This style had come from Rome by way of Inigo Jones and Sir Christopher Wren.

Philadelphia grew quickly. Within two years it had more than 350 houses. The little "Letitia Street House" is the best example known of the very early Quaker dwellings. Though other houses were more pretentious and many were certainly less so, this one is probably typical of the home of a prosperous artisan or a small merchant. It had but four rooms and an attic (there may have been a separate kitchen out back) but it was neatly built of brick, with painted woodwork, and in its windows were some of the first sash in America that slid up and down. It takes no study of architecture to see at a glance that this is a totally different kind of structure from either the timber houses that had served New England or the brick ones of the South.

Inside, each of the four rooms had a fireplace angled in a corner, all four served by the same large chimney. Between the front and back rooms there was a winding stair, narrow and without ornamentation as was the Quaker way. The inside walls were plastered and whitewashed. The furniture was walnut or oak and not designed for relaxing, but it was nicely made and some of it was handsome.

There was never any "starving time" in Pennsylvania. The population increased rapidly. Phila-

The Letitia Street House in Philadelphia

Pennsylvania German house of hewn logs

delphia grew to have 14,000 people in eighteen years, and nearly all of them were more prosperous than they had ever been before. Germans made up the bulk of the increase, though the majority of these spread into the back country.

German Settlers

The actual circumstances of their immigration make a horror story. Many were so poor that they had to mortage their own labor and that of their children to pay for passage. The passage they bought was so dreadfully bad that hundreds of them died at sea. Diseases often appeared on ship-

board and then the voyage ended in a nightmare quarantine of weeks at anchor in the river. This wasn't improved by the fact that neither the ship's captain nor the shore authorities felt any obligation to feed the passengers. They were dependent on what they could buy or what private charity provided.

The Germans were the best farmers in the Colonies, the most industrious, and the thriftiest. Alone of all the colonists, they avoided girdling trees. They cut them, and what wood they didn't need for building log cabins they split into fence rails and firewood, and stored. Their barns were usually larger and finer than their houses. They overdid the thrift, sacrificing not only luxury but even comfort to gain profit. It was said of them in derision that they fed their pigs and gave what was left to their families.

German Houses

The German log houses came to be better built than the original Swedish ones that they copied. The first improvement was to hew the tops and bottoms of the logs flat, for closer fit. Later they used squared timbers as logs. For a neater appearance, they trimmed off the projecting ends of the logs at the corners of the house and went on to

The main room of a Pennsylvania German farmhouse

form tighter joints there, where log rested on log, angling the cuts of the joints so that water would run out of them. It's possible that these people brought the knowledge of how to do this with them to this country, for hewn-log houses existed in parts of Germany.

Some of the German houses were half-timber, framed and diagonally braced with hewn beams and with the spaces filled with brick or stone nogging. By the middle of the eighteenth century they favored houses with thick field-stone walls. Usually they built them into the side of a hill as they did their "bank" barns. Often these houses were built over a spring and the cellar was used as a milk-cooling room. This evidently wasn't done to provide water in case of Indian attack, because there was never any inside access to the cellar. Very often a German settler would mount an iron silhouette of an Indian on the roof as a sign that he had paid the natives for his land.

Though these were simple houses for simple farm living, their interiors were often quite elaborately finished, and the kitchen, which was the principal living room of the house, might have fine paneling in it and a stair with a carved banister that would have served for a mansion. Plastered walls were usually whitewashed, and the furniture was likely to have brightly painted decorations on it, usually involving tulips and birds.

The Scotch-Irish

One other large group came to Pennsylvania, beginning early in the eighteenth century, continuing all through it, and spreading into other colonies until it is said that they formed one-sixth of the population. These were the Scotch-Irish and the Scotch-Scots, mostly spinners and weavers by trade. Most of the coastal land had been taken up and they had to head for the back country. A good many of those who came into Pennsylvania "snuck" in by the back door. They came to Maryland by sea and followed the Susquehanna River into the Cumberland and Juniata valleys; the route was shorter and they avoided formalities.

These people were by temperament the utter antithesis of Quaker calm and of German thrift. They took the land they wanted and dared anybody to move them; seldom did anyone do so. They were fiercely independent and stubbornly belligerent. It is said that when the break came with England, there was not even one Tory to be found among the Scotch-Irish. They despised the Indians, seeing them only as heathens to be exterminated. Naturally the Indians reciprocated and raided them, early and often. A state of war existed so continuously that children born into it accepted it as the normal condition of life and couldn't imagine it ever ending.

Log Forts and Cabins

For protection these frontiersmen grouped their small farms around "forts" built where three or four cabins were close together and where a good spring could be enclosed. The forts were nothing more than log fences with one or more blockhouses as places of last resort. There are towns, now, where many of these strong points stood.

The log cabin was ideally suited to the wilder-

A frontier fort in western Pennsylvania

Puncheon table and benches

and sometimes it hadn't even that, the entrance being on the upper level, reached by a ladder that could be drawn up. Unfortunately the whole structure was made of wood and, if the Indians had the luck of dry weather, the roof could be ignited with fire arrows.

Customs and Trade

All through the summer these people were constantly on guard. When cold weather settled in, the Indians holed up in their lodges and let the whites alone. But often in late November there would be a warm spell and a sudden attack would be staged. So it is, they say, that such a warm spell in autumn came to be called Indian summer.

When a community building job was finished, everybody celebrated with an all-night dance, feasted on potpie, and got drunk on homemade whisky. This commodity may have been introduced into America by the Scotch-Irish, who certainly brought with them the knowledge of how to make it. They made lots of it. Transportation difficulties ruled out selling excess grain in bulk but, reduced to liquor, it could be taken to market quite easily. Nobody bothered with tea or coffee; they had to be carried too far and they were despised as "slops" that didn't stick to your ribs. Table furniture, as they called it, was mostly homemade woodenware (treen ware) of the sort we discussed earlier in New England. Occasionally somebody would own a pewter spoon or two.

The frontiersman did little farming at first. Mostly he lived by hunting, but he had to "import" a few things, like salt and iron, and to buy the horses that were his only means of bringing them from the coast. In addition to his whisky and the pelts he accumulated, he made alum as trade

ness, so these settlers adopted it from the Germans and clung to it long after the Germans gave it up. When one was to be erected, a whole community would turn out, fell the timber, and finish the house in three days, including the split clapboard roof and the puncheon floor. A puncheon floor was made of half logs, with their flat sides upward, made as level and splinterless as could be managed with an ax. Puncheons made the tops of tables and benches also. The journey from the coast was too difficult for anyone to be able to bring in any "joiner's work" and adzes were barely less scarce than was the skill to use them.

Blockhouses were log structures. They were usually built of squared logs with tight corners and a minimum of projections, to discourage climbing. The standard blockhouse design was two stories high, with the second floor projecting over the first on all four sides. Loopholes, to shoot through, were made in the floor of the overhang, as well as in the second-story walls. The lower story usually had no openings except one heavy door,

An alum train in the mountains

goods. He burned wood, leached the ashes, and boiled down the residue, chipping the alum off the pot. Two bushels of alum weighed 168 pounds and made a load for one pack horse; one bushel of it could be traded in a town for a cow and a calf. Often the trading town was one to the south, because it was easier to follow the valleys than to cross the ridges. The pack trains were originally organized as community affairs but, later, individuals went into the transportation business and operated private caravans. Each horse was belled so that he could be found after a night's stop. It would never do to *buy* food supplies in town, so enough food was loaded for the entire trip, both ways. Some was dropped off and hidden on the way down, to be picked up on the way back.

Clothes

We have been educated to think of the frontiersman as wearing a caped and fringed hunting shirt of leather, but apparently his shirt, though fringed and caped, was made of leather only when nothing else was available. It was rough linen in summer and linsey-woolsey in winter. Wet leather makes about as uncomfortable a garment as can be hung on the human frame, and the woodsman was often wet. His shirt was long; it hung halfway down his thighs. It was open down the front and confined by a belt or, more properly, a cincture,

tied in the back. Hanging from the belt was a tomahawk on the right, a knife on the left, and a bullet bag in front. The shirt was lapped far over in front to make a capacious pocket for bread, jerked meat, rifle tow, and tobacco. At his right side a large pouch hung from a shoulder strap. In it were carried lead and a mold for bullets, and flint and steel. Tied to the same shoulder strap, above the pouch, was the powder horn. Sometimes the hunter wore leg-length leggings that looked like close-fitting pants; as often, he wore only high moccasins, with their tops tied around his leg below the knee, and an Indian-style breechclout, leaving the upper part of his leg bare. In cold weather he stuffed deer hair or dry leaves into his moccasins to keep his feet warm.

People

These were simple, violent people, much given to horseplay, to running and jumping contests, and to bare-fisted fighting and gouging. At a wedding, which was a three-day celebration, the girls put the bride to bed with all ceremony, then the men grabbed the groom and forcibly put him into the bed with her! Anything like thieving called for an on-the-spot investigation and immediate punishment. For questioning the suspect was "sweated." His arms were pinioned behind him and he was suspended by them from a tree

Frontier justice

until he had told all. If it was decided he was guilty, he was at once flogged, with a hickory rod, "nineteen to the dozen," by everybody present, and released. There was no place to lock up anybody, nor with all the work that had to be done could a man be spared if there had been.

"Shootin' Arns" and Game

After the ax, and sometimes before it, the gun was the most important implement on the frontier. The woodsmen early admired the heavy rifles the Germans had brought with them, which, though their weight made them worthless in the woods, could outshoot any musket in distance and accuracy. There were good gunsmiths among the Germans and they were persuaded to make a lighter rifle, one that could be loaded, without the use of a mallet, by wrapping an undersized lead ball in a leather patch and shoving patch and ball together into the barrel. This gun was fired by a flintlock, a vast improvement over the old firelock. Men took it over the mountains later, into the "dark and bloody ground," and it somehow became known as the Kentucky rifle, but it was a Pennsylvania rifle for a long time before that. Shooting it constantly, the frontiersmen became prodigiously good at knocking the eyes out of squirrels at a hundred yards. A shooting match with a "kag" of whisky or a rifle as the prize for the best score was the central feature of every gathering.

There was game everywhere and there were "varmints" such as wolves, and wildcats, and snakes. It wasn't unusual for a man to kill half a dozen copperheads and rattlers in the course of mowing a small field. Even edible animals were varmints when they destroyed crops. Nobody had yet given a thought to conservation, so, to thin the animal population, the settlers held game drives in which all the animals, regardless of kind, were herded into some small valley and ruthlessly slaughtered. The drives did nothing to increase the white man's popularity with the Indians but they cleaned out nearly all the animals that couldn't burrow or fly.

II. THE COASTAL COLONIES

Agriculture

Throughout the eighteenth century, the colonists depended on farming as their chief means of income. In spite of the Pennsylvania Germans, it can't be said that the Americans generally were good farmers. They mined the land rather than farmed it. With the trees removed, the good topsoil washed away and started filling the streams and harbors with mud. Most of the coastal land was worn out thirty years before the Revolution. By 1700 one group or another had introduced nearly all of the common fruits and garden vegetables. Corn was native, so were sweet potatoes, as far north as the Eastern Shore of Maryland. Irish potatoes were brought in from the West Indies, either directly or by way of the British Isles, first to Virginia and in 1718 to New England. They were a curiosity at first, used as an ornamental garnish for meat. Potatoes had another use also: a small one, carried in a pocket, was considered sure protection against rheumatism.

Grains were the most profitable things to raise, always excepting tobacco when the market wasn't flooded. In the Middle Colonies, wheat could be ground into flour and sold both north and south. Much flour came to be shipped overseas too, though little of it went to England because of restrictions. By the middle of the eighteenth century the little town of Baltimore had become the world's principal flour milling and shipping center. Great fortunes were made growing rice in the soggy flatlands along the South Carolina coast and shipping it to Europe. A New England ship captain named John Thurber started the South Carolinians growing rice by bringing some seed to Charleston in 1668. Two years later 330 tons were shipped.

Rice has to do its growing under a few inches of

water. It was a simple matter to dam a sluggish stream above tidewater and flood the land along its swampy banks. No clearing had to be done; the marshes grew nothing but grass and rushes. Work in the rice fields was done entirely by slave labor. Plants were started in seedbeds and transplanted by hand to the muck in which they were to grow. The only tool needed was a hoe. The water was drained off when the grain began to ripen, and the straw was cut with sickles. Mules, used to bring the harvested rice in from the fields, had to be shod with broad-soled, wooden boots to keep them from sinking in the mud. Once on solid ground, rice was handled like any other grain. It was threshed with flails and winnowed by the wind, when it was poured from high platforms built for the purpose.

Wood and Wooden Implements

Implements for the more normal kinds of farming continued to be made by the user or by the

Hickory-lashed harrow, made with no metal whatever

local blacksmith. For the most part they were similar to those used in the previous century but some improvements were made. Plows were a little less ponderous and more of them had iron shares. Seldom did a harrow have iron teeth, however; big oak, or hickory, pegs served the purpose. They were either wedged into holes made in a heavy log frame, or they were lashed into place on a lighter frame with strips of green hickory that shrank when they dried and gripped the teeth immovably. A few of these hickory-lashed harrows still survive, with their teeth as tightly fixed as they ever were.

Each kind of wood has its own characteristics and, in a time when wood was the all-purpose material, people acquired a wide knowledge of the kinds that would best serve particular uses. Lacking iron, black gum (tupelo) would make the best plowshare, because its tortuous grain made it almost impossible to split. If you needed toughness and springiness, there was hickory, with ash as a second choice, though ash was usually preferred for ax handles. White oak was used where great strength was needed, as for treenails and the timbers of ships. Cedar was light and strong and was little hurt by water; it was perfect for small boats and for piggins, and pails, and shingles. Chestnut, too, resisted weather well; it made fine fence rails, but it wasn't much good for firewood, because, burning, it would pop sparks all over a room. Modern cabinetmakers shudder at the fact that black walnut was also used for fence rails. Locust, almost impervious to rot, made the best fence posts. White pine, strong but soft and easily worked, was for clapboards and for the masts of ships, for interior paneling, and for chair seats. Alder made good charcoal for gunpowder. The list goes on to include almost every native tree, large and small.

To come back to wooden farm implements: The old, split-and-spread hay fork remained in use but it more often had four tines than three. Other forms of forks appeared that would pick up more hay, or handle special materials. Five or six tines were set into a transverse bar and some forks had a low fence on the top of the bar against which the stuff being handled could stack up. Wooden hand-rakes six feet wide were used in the hayfield. So were wooden horse-rakes, so made that a man, walking behind, could flip one over and dump the load without stopping the horse.

Farm Animals

Oxen remained the principal working animals. Stronger and less nervous than horses, they were ideal for farm work at a time when haste wasn't popular. We don't see many of them now and when we do we usually see them in pairs, but our forefathers often worked a single ox, using a special yoke, of course. It's necessary to protect the feet of working oxen with iron shoes, just as a horse is shod; but, since the hoof of an ox is cloven, each shoe must be made in two pieces. Oxen are heavy and their feet are small; because of this, an ox can't stand on three feet and hold up the fourth for the farrier, as a horse can.

When an ox was shod, he had to be stood in a special stanchion equipped with slings that passed under his belly. By raising the slings with a windlass and a series of overhead pulleys or rollers, the smith could lift the animal enough to take the excess weight off its feet. The operation was hard on the ox. Farmers said one shoeing hurt their oxen more than a week of hard work.

Though horses filled fewer working needs than did oxen on Colonial farms, they could be ridden and hence were desirable. Twenty-nine Flanders mares and three Dutch stallions were brought to the Massachusetts Bay Colony in 1635 and horses came steadily to all the Colonies from then on. Thoroughbreds were imported after 1700 in some quantity, and a few ran on American turf before that. The first known piece of American silversmithing was a prize for a horse race.

Two distinctive American breeds of horse appeared in the eighteenth century and vanished again, no doubt leaving traces of their blood behind them. The Narragansett Pacer was a riding horse of Spanish extraction, small, hardy, and, because of his side-winding gait, very comfortable. The Conestoga horse, said to have had English an-

Wooden hay fork with a "fence"

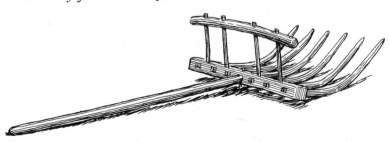

106

Ox in a sling, for shoeing.
The inset shows the two halves of an ox shoe

cestry, despite the fact that he flourished among the Pennsylvania Germans, developed in time to pull the famous wagons of the same name and lasted until the railroads put him, and them, out of business in the nineteenth century. He was usually black and, understandably, he was big, strong, and steady.

In most of the Colonies the law allowed farm animals to roam at large and gave anyone who objected the right to fence them out. However, some preferred to keep their own animals enclosed. These people restrained the tendency to jump fences, or to break through them, by fitting their beasts with a variety of yokes and "pokes." A yoke,

Sheep wearing a yoke

A cow poke

Bee gum and straw skip

something of contentment from their humming. They furnished a cheap substitute for sugar and, even if that hadn't been valued, they would have earned their small keep by pollinating fruit trees. Northern bees were hived in braided straw "skips" usually capped with a loose straw thatch. In the South, perhaps because less insulation was needed, the "bee gum" became the traditional hive. It was actually a hollow section of a gum tree, provided with a movable lid. Both skip and gum were set on a bench, or some other support, to keep them off the damp ground. When cold weather slowed the bees down, there was a great excitement in further stupefying them with the smoke of burning rags and making off with their reserve supply of honey.

Pork

No matter how small the farm, it always had a few pigs. They were easy to feed and maintain and they provided the mainstay of the winter's provi-

in this sense, was a simple frame hung around the neck. Its extensions served to catch on palings or rails and to prevent a sheep, a goose, or even a hen from squeezing through a fence. Pokes also hung around an animal's neck but they carried a rod, poking forward, to catch in a fence if any jumping was attempted.

Bees must be rated as domestic animals. Nearly every farm had them, North or South, and gained

Scalding and scraping hogs

sions. The first really frosty weather signaled hog killin'. Outside, long before the first light of a crackling cold dawn, a huge iron kettle was filled with water and had a roaring fire built under it that lighted up the farmstead. The water was boiling by sunrise, and the men took a sharp knife to the pigpen, to do what had to be done. Many a gentle wife sat in the kitchen, with her hands over her ears, until the slaughter was over and the carcasses had been hauled on a pung (sled) to the side of the fire. Using tackle hung from a tripod, the body of a hog was heaved up and lowered into the boiling pot; then out again and onto a wooden rack, where the hair was scraped off with bell-shaped scrapers. Not every farmer owned a hog-size kettle, but a barrel could be made to serve. Water in a barrel was heated by the old Indian method of throwing hot stones (or hot scrap iron) into it. This system is probably still used; it certainly has been used within the last ten years.

Pennsylvania bank barn

The carcass was emptied, beheaded, and halved, and then taken into the kitchen, where the women, usually helped by neighbors, waded into the business of processing it. Fat was cut away and rendered into lard, and everybody chewed on the "cracklin's" that floated to the top of the lard kettle. The back meat was chopped up for sausage (this was before the days of grinders), seasoned, and stuffed into skins (intestines) for smoking. Some of the sausage meat was kept out to be eaten fresh, and this was traditionally shared with all the neighbors.

Hams, shoulders, and bacon went into a barrel of brine, "strong enough to float an egg," for corning, before they were smoked. Heads and feet were cooked at once, and the meat from them was mixed with vinegar and spices and made into "head cheese" and "souse." The livers were cooked, too, and chopped fine for "pudding" that might be stirred into corn-meal mush and cooled in pans as "scrapple." The last of the job was done in candlelight, and the final "redding up" of the kitchen was likely to be left for next morning.

Barns and Houses

Most of the first American barns had thatched roofs and a few were covered that way for a long

Connected house and barn in New England

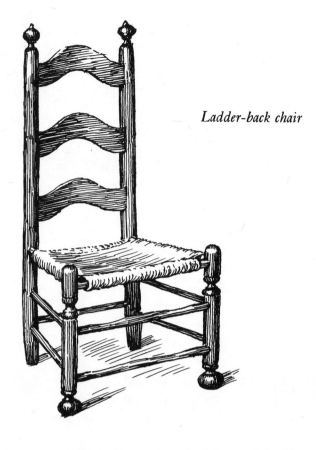

Ladder-back chair

the new, all-wood, sliding sash to supplant the ancient casements. People began to be interested in placing windows symmetrically in walls, and doorways began to acquire ornamental frames and glazed transoms. Roofs changed too; fewer of them were quite so steep and more of them, especially in the South, began to have the gambrel shape that gave more room in the attic.

Most attics were used as sleeping quarters, and they were pretty dark and stuffy when their only openings were little windows in the gable ends. The new way of building used upright windows, called dormers, each with a small roof of its own, let into the slope of the main roof of a house. The idea was seized on as a godsend and dormers were put in old roofs as well as new ones. Taverns, needing many small sleeping rooms, soon presented an unbroken row of dormers, set like saw teeth the full length of the roof.

Interiors

It was natural that, when some sense of security and permanence came to the colonists, they would begin to dress up the interiors of their houses. Country-made furniture had become lighter by the beginning of the eighteenth century and had acquired an awkward grace, if not much comfort. A banister-back chair had to be made by an expert who had a lathe, but a somewhat similar chair, with plain vertical slats in its back, could be achieved at home. High-backed chairs, with or without arms and with horizontal back slats often arched upward, are called "ladder-backs." They were made on the place and their seats were woven of rushes or of split hickory. A smart Yankee, or a clever Southern slave, could make one, rounding the legs and stretchers with a spokeshave.

The early settlers had been content to cover their walls either with whitewashed plaster or with simple sheathing boards, usually applied vertically but sometimes put on horizontally. In an effort to make the boards more attractive, carpenters began to cut moldings on their edges. Down South these were quite narrow and simple, but up North the craftsman shaped a special plane blade that would produce a deep molding, sometimes as much as two inches wide, made up of several ridges and grooves.

time, especially in Pennsylvania. Many of the big Pennsylvania barns had stone ends and almost all of them were built into a south-facing bank. The arrangement served the double purposes of keeping the foundation floor warm for the stock and allowing a hay wagon to drive onto the loft floor above. Corn shocks were stacked against the exposed parts of the foundation for additional warmth in winter.

Barns in all the Middle Colonies were "out behind the house," at no great distance. In Virginia they were likely to be scattered all over the place, and none of them was usually very large. Up in New England, where deep snow was to be expected, barns and houses were connected by way of a woodshed attached to the lean-to kitchen; mostly they still are. The barn in those parts might be set at a right angle to the house so that the angle between them made a sheltered courtyard.

The new styles of building houses that were appearing in the towns slowly had their effect on the appearance of farmhouses, even though each section tended to cling to its old ways. In the North the saltbox house was as popular as ever, but the lean-to was invariably an integral part of the structure. In a country where wood was infinitely more plentiful than lead, it was common sense for

Fireplace wall with hip-raised panels

The next enrichment was "hip-raised" paneling. There was nothing new about it, but nobody had time for such fripperies at first. Wide, usually rather short boards were chamfered all the way around and framed with narrow boards that had moldings cut on their edges. Ordinary panel doors are made this way now, but the "hips" of the panels aren't made as high as they used to be, nor are the chamfers as wide. At first only the wall around the keeping-room fireplace was likely to be paneled; later all four walls were done. In big houses, the whole first floor was paneled and often the second-floor bedrooms as well.

The earliest paneling, like the older sheathing, was left bare, with no finish except what time would give it, and time has done a fine job. Oil paint began to be used in Virginia about the beginning of the eighteenth century, on both the outsides and the insides of houses. It became customary to paint wood paneling, and those who couldn't get oil paint used the sour-milk kind that could be stirred up at home. Many an old wall and mantel, laboriously cleaned of paint by modern "restorers," has had its wood exposed for the first time since it was put in place.

Plantations

Up the Hudson and on the Southern rivers, wealthy landowners built themselves elaborate country houses in the new style. Except that they spread out more, these were much like the houses the same people and others equally rich built for themselves in towns. Southern plantation houses

A plantation house, early eighteenth century

Ha-ha wall

To reduce the amount of cutting, sheep, which crop grass very closely, were generally pastured between the house and the river. But it was undesirable to have the animals too close to the house, and a fence to keep them away would have spoiled the sweep of the "fall" to the water. The ha-ha wall provided a solution. A wide ditch about two feet deep was dug across the lawn and a wall was built in it, against its uphill side. The top of the wall was invisible from the house, but a sheep, wandering into the ditch, couldn't get over it. An unsuspecting stranger could fall into the ditch, however, and sometimes did.

The plantations operated as self-sufficient units except for their importations of luxuries from England. Most plantations did their own spinning and weaving and all of the ordinary needs of the retainers were met by the production of the place itself. Nomini Hall, in Virginia, had at one time eleven carpenters, two joiners, a brickmaker, a bricklayer, a blacksmith, a miller, a tanner, a shoemaker, a hatter, a sailor, a carter, a coachman, no doubt a schoolmaster, and certainly an overseer. What the total population was, including field slaves and house servants, is left to the imagination. Some notion can be formed from an account of the food and drink consumed on another plantation, Carter's Grove, where in one year family, guests, and "help" used 27,000 pounds of pork, 20 beeves, 550 bushels of grain, over 500 gallons of rum (four hogsheads), and 150 gallons of brandy.

often had wings at both ends. Actually these were separate buildings. At first they were completely detached or were connected to the main house only by covered walkways. Later the walkway became an enclosed passage, except in a very few cases, like that of Mt. Vernon. One of the small end-buildings was usually a kitchen; the other served as an office for the Master.

Surrounding a plantation house was a wide stretch of lawn, usually reaching to the water's edge on one side and to the House Gate on the other. The Entrance Gate was likely to be a mile or more away. There were no lawn mowers to keep grass shorn to an even, velvety length. Any cutting had to be done with scythes, but even an expert couldn't make it much shorter than three inches, and the evenness left much to be desired, unless you had never seen it done better.

INDUSTRIES

Iron

In all the Colonies, fishing, trapping, and lumbering occupied many men but, like farming and the trades, were individual enterprises. There were also a few real industries that required the services of a number of men working together. The most important of these were the "furnaces" where crude ore was smelted down to pig iron, and the forges where it was further refined and improved. The British urged the Americans to smelt ore but discouraged and tried to prohibit them from making it up into anything. On the eastern side of the Atlantic, it was felt that colonies should be a source of supply for the parent country's needs and a profitable market for its products.

Even as early as Roanoke Island, the settlers found iron ore. It was of the sort called "bog iron" that was said to "grow" in ponds; lumps of it were fished up with long-handled tongs. There seems to have been quite a supply. One New England pond yielded more than 300 tons a year for sixty years.

The earliest attempt to smelt this iron was in Virginia. It failed because of Indian trouble. The Puritans did better, at Lynn, with a furnace that seems to have been little more than a large fireplace. It partly melted but didn't liquefy the ore. Though the result could be beaten into rough bars, they were too poor in quality to be rolled into sheets or drawn into wire. A better furnace was started at near-by Saugus in 1646. It used air to blow up a hot fire and produced eight tons a week of iron good enough to make into pots and mortars and to be forged into wrought-iron bars. The Saugus ironworks has been meticulously restored to its original appearance with the help of the American Iron and Steel Institute.

Furnaces multiplied in the Colonies in the eighteenth century, notably in Connecticut, New Jersey, Pennsylvania, Maryland, and Virginia. In form they were sturdy stone towers built with sloping walls, on a rectangular foundation. A chimney rose from the center to a total height of about thirty feet. The tower enclosed a roughly egg-shaped chamber into which fuel, ore, and flux could be dumped in layers from a platform, and from the bottom of which molten iron could be run off into sand molds to form pigs. The furnace fires were blown with big double bellows, worked by water power. The flux was oyster shells or limestone and served to release impurities from the ore.

All of the Southern furnaces and a few of the Northern ones were manned by slaves, some of whom became expert at specialized jobs. It took up to 120 slaves to run a furnace, we are told; presumably that didn't include mining the ore. Ore for the Principio furnace, at the head of Chesapeake Bay, was brought fifty miles in boats that had double banks of oars pulled by white convict redemptioners.

The fuel of all the furnaces was charcoal, and it was cutting wood to make it that, far more than agriculture, denuded the Eastern seaboard of its forests. Four square miles of woodland was considered necessary as the basic supply for setting up a furnace.

Charcoal

Charcoal-burning became an industry in itself. The material was produced by burning wood, with a restricted supply of air, to evaporate nearly all its water, drive off unwanted gases, and leave it more or less pure carbon. The wood was cut into short billets, stacked on the ground or in pits, covered with earth, and burned from the center outward. A "chimney" was left in the middle of the heap, to be closed when combustion was well

Charcoal-burning

started. There were draft vents at the bottom of the pile to be closed or opened as the state of the burning and the direction and strength of the wind required.

For the first few days the whole mound steamed. As burning progressed, vent holes had to be made in the walls of the pile to release gases, otherwise the whole thing might explode. When the coaling reached a certain point, determined by the diminished size of the heap and by probing, all openings were closed and the earth covering was sealed by wetting it down and keeping it wet for eight or ten days. The whole burning took several weeks of day-and-night watching and sometimes strenuous emergency action.

Tanbark and Leather

Tanbark should have been a by-product of charcoal-burning, since bark was of no value for coaling. But trees were too plentiful for anybody to worry about waste, so oaks, hemlocks, and firs were cut for their bark only. It was stripped off the trees and crushed into shreds under a toothed stone wheel operated by ox-power. Crushed bark was sold to the tanners in bales or by the load.

Tanners were busy everywhere at their smelly trade. Leather served all the purposes for which we now use it and also was used in places where we now use rubber and plastics. Leather breeches took a lot of it; carriages were slung on leather

A tanbark mill

Glass blowers at the "glory hole"

"thoroughbraces"; many people wore boots; many more rode on leather saddles and drove horses hitched with leather harness. The tanners used quantities of bark which they steeped in water to extract the tannic acid that cured their hides and skins. It took a full year to turn a new hide into good leather: removing the hair, scraping the inside, soaking and turning in the tanning vats, and currying to smoothness and softness.

Glass

Glass, especially for windows, was in great demand in the Colonies, so it was one of the things the British taxed without representation. Most of the glass produced here seems to have been made by Germans. The Dutch made some in New Amsterdam in 1654, but Germans were brought in for an attempt to make glass in Massachusetts. Caspar Wistar of Philadelphia, who was the first to make a commercial success at it in 1739, was a German; so was the flamboyant "Baron" Stiegel, who qual-

ified, much later, as the greatest American glassmaker. Wistar made bottles and window glass, with brass buttons, "guaranteed to last seven years," as a side line.

A Colonial glassmaker cooked the sand, soda ash, and lime that made his product in a beehive-shaped clay pot that had an arched opening near its top from which the glass could be taken a little at a time. The fundamental tool for making anything of glass was a metal tube, about five feet long, called a "blowing rod." On one end of this the blower gathered a lump of molten material from the pot. It was gummy and thick in consistency, and he blew it into a glass bubble by lung power. What he did with the bubble after it was blown determined what article he would produce.

Window glass was made in circular sheets, called crown glass. The blower transferred his bubble to a solid rod, called a "punty," which he rested in a forked support before an open furnace, called the "glory hole." When the glass was very soft, he spun the rod between his hands. Centrif-

Eighteenth-century blown glassware

ugal force flattened the bubble. Its front and back surfaces met and stuck together and it was still kept hot and rotated until it became a wide thin disk. Skill was needed to keep this pancake distended until it had cooled enough to hold its shape. When it had, the rod was snapped off, leaving a thick lump of rough glass, called a "bull's-eye." The center pane cut from the sheet retained the lump and was sold as bull's-eye glass, the cheapest there was. But before the sheet could be

Glass blower's chair

cut, it had to be annealed. This was done (it still is) by cooling very slowly in an oven; otherwise the glass would develop internal stresses that would cause it to shatter at a touch.

Panes cut from the outer parts of the crown-glass disk were of top quality, better than the "sheet" glass that began to be made, about 1800, by slitting an elongated bubble and opening it out flat.

The older the glass, the smaller the panes cut from it. In medieval times the crown-glass disk was so small that it would yield only a single bull's-eye pane. In the early seventeenth century, quarrels, about four inches square, were cut from the outer parts of the crown. Wistar, in addition to smaller stock sizes, offered to make special sheets sixteen inches by eighteen.

Bottles and drinking glasses could be made by manipulating the glass bubble into shape, in which case the result was a "blown" bottle; or the bubble could be inflated inside a metal mold, this resulted in "pressed" glass. The molds were made in two or three pieces. Little seams show on the surface of pressed glass where the mold edges met.

To make a blown-glass bottle, the worker evened up the blob of glass on his rod by rolling it on an iron table before he started to blow. After it was blown, the bubble was transferred with the help of an assistant from the blowing rod to a punty. The punty was laid across the iron-covered arms of a special chair on which the glass-blower seated himself. Rolling the rod on the arms, the blower could overcome any sagging of the hot material. He worked beyond one arm, grasping the glass and shaping it with wooden tools as his skill and fancy allowed. When it became too cool for working, it was reheated at the glory hole.

Paper

Paper was so scarce in the Colonies at first as to be almost absent. A paper mill was started at Germantown in 1690 by William Rittenhouse, who had learned his trade in Holland. His mill was on a river, since plenty of clean water was one of the two things essential to the making of paper. Water was needed in the product and also to turn a wheel for power. The other necessary thing was linen rags. Cotton, wood, and some other materials can be used for paper, but the early Ameri-

A paper mill.
The equipment is bunched up, so as to show most of it in one drawing

cans stuck to linen and made very good paper from it.

The rags were washed, cut into bits, and boiled with lye until the cloth had disintegrated; then the lye was washed away. The remaining mass was beaten in a mill until not only had all vestige of cloth vanished, but the thread was gone also and the flax was reduced to a pulp of its basic fibers. The "stuff," as it was called, was moved then to a warmed vat from which it could be dipped to be turned into paper. When it was ready to use, the stuff had about the consistency of pancake batter, and it needed to be stirred to keep it from settling.

The dipping was done with a rectangular sieve, called a mold. The bottom of the sieve was made of taut wires, rather heavy ones across the short dimension, with much lighter ones running lengthwise. The pattern of these wires was impressed permanently in the paper, as was the maker's "watermark," which was formed of wire and fastened to the upper surface of the sieve.

Before dipping the moldman placed a loose wooden frame in the mold. This was called the "deckle." It served to limit the size of the sheet and to prevent the new paper from adhering to the edges of the mold. The mold was submerged edgewise in the vat, turned, and brought up flat. As he

brought it to the surface, the moldman gave the mold a double shake that crossed the fibers and made them cling together.

The bulk of the water drained out as the mold was lifted from the vat, but far too much remained to allow the sheet to be touched. The moldman removed the deckle, making a clean, but irregular, cut on all four edges of his sheet. The mold was then taken by the coucher, who deftly dumped its contents onto a felt pad, the top one of a stack of such pads, each supporting a sheet of paper.

When a "post" of 144 sheets had accumulated, the pile was moved to the "wet press" and then squeezed as hard as possible to get more water out. The lone man working at this in the illustration is a mere symbol; it actually required the combined efforts of everybody on the place. After this compression, the damp paper was strong enough to be lifted from the felts by hand and it was stacked in the "dry press" for more, but much lighter, squeezing. Then it was hung over cow-hair ropes, in "spurs" of four or five sheets, to dry in the air. Cow hair was used because it didn't stain the paper. The product still had to be dipped in gelatin to "size" it, redried, and then given a surface glaze. This last finishing could be done by hand with an agate burnisher, but at the beginning of

the eighteenth century it was usually put under a big water-powered hammer. In later years it was run through wooden rollers. Rittenhouse charged twenty shillings a ream for writing paper; this may be guessed at the equivalent of about fifteen dollars.

Colonial printers turned out their news sheets, "almanacks," pamphlets, and an occasional book on hand presses that differed but little from the press on which Johannes Gutenberg first printed the Bible. Their working parts were iron but the heavy frames, braced between floor and ceiling, were made entirely of wood.

The lead type was cast in hand-cut brass molds, each letter on its own small block. The characters showed some irregularity but surprisingly little, considering the difficulties of shaping a minute recess in a block of brass. Reading them backwards and upside down, the printer set up his letters one by one in a small brass pan he called a stick. He checked his accuracy with a rough proof obtained by rubbing or tapping the back of a piece of scrap paper placed on the inked type. The next step was to wedge the type into an iron frame called a form. The method of doing this was improved later; sometimes Colonial type slipped a bit and wandered off the line.

The type form lay on the bed of the press and could be slid out for inking. Gummy ink was applied with a stuffed leather dauber. A sheet of dampened paper was placed carefully on the inked type and held there by a hinged frame that pressed upon its edges. Type and paper were slid into the press and the heavy iron platen was squeezed down upon them by means of a steep-pitched screw turned by a longish handle.

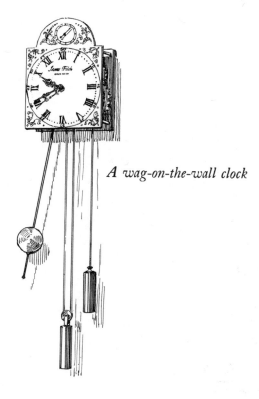

A wag-on-the-wall clock

Clocks

The mechanical bent that the soil of New England generated in its sons led some of them to an interest in clock mechanisms and, by 1710, they were making clocks for sale to their fellow townsmen. At first a clockmaker made and sold "works" only. A purchaser had to have his clock case made elsewhere, by a joiner. Cases were expensive and the clock, being provided by its maker with a face, would tell time in the nude, so many people did without a case, simply hanging up the mechanism. This kind of bare clock was known as a "wag-on-the-wall," from the motion of its pendulum, swinging in full view.

Being always short of metal, the Yankees carved wooden gears for many of their clocks. It seems almost miraculous that some of these should still be counting time after a couple of centuries, but they are. Except that some clocks had larger faces and works and longer pendulums than others, a clock

mechanism could be put into any kind of case; so some were shelf clocks, and some were wall clocks, and still others stood on the floor in seven-foot cases and marked not only the time, but also the phases of the moon. These were grandfather clocks, of course. There were also grandmother clocks. These, too, stood on the floor, but they were a couple of feet shorter.

Vehicles and Roads

The building of wagons and carriages could scarcely be called an industry, but it was a steadily increasing occupation. Most blacksmiths were also wheelwrights and turned a hand at "ironing" carts and wagons, or constructed entire vehicles in their shops. In the larger centers there were men who worked on vehicles exclusively.

Every farm needed a cart, and many were used for dray work in towns. As the population of the Allegheny settlements increased, the bulk of their products and their needs did also, and the pack train no longer sufficed to carry them. The Pennsylvania Germans evolved the great Conestoga wagon to serve the Western trade and also to haul their own farm products down to tidewater. These wagons were an adaptation of those the settlers were familiar with in Europe. They were high and heavy, and extremely strong, as they had to be, to run on trails that had been improved only to the extent of removing the obstacles that couldn't be by-passed. The Conestoga body curved upward at both ends and its sides sloped outward, so that a load tended to settle toward the bottom and the middle.

The larger wagons were drawn by eight horses, controlled by a single jerkline and half a dozen verbal commands. In the tradition of the pack

A Conestoga wagon

A chair or shay

trains, an iron hoop hung with bells was mounted above the collar of each animal, except that of the left-hand horse nearest the wagon; he was saddled and the driver ordinarily rode on him. There was normally a second man along who walked beside the wagon or rode the "lazyboard" and operated the long-handled brake. The "waggoners" camped at night, feeding their horses from a long trough, which was set on the tongue of the wagon at mealtimes and slung behind the body in transit. The horses were hobbled for the night to keep them near-by. Gradually life grew a little more comfortable for the wagon men as the roads improved from sheer use and crude inns were opened along them.

The streets of towns along the coast were extended to become local roads. A need for carriages appeared and the "wonderful one-hoss shay" was born. South of Boston it was called a "chair" or, more often, a "cheer." It had as an ancestor the *chaise* of the French, but the American version was a tougher affair, with innovations that were entirely native. Chief among them were the hickory springs from which the back of the body was suspended. A country "cheer" either had no top, or it had an immovable one of canvas. When it moved to town and became a "chair," the whole carriage was better finished; it was painted and was given a collapsible calash top of leather. The chair in the illustration is town-bred.

One other passenger vehicle appeared in the eighteenth century that seems to have been wholly American in origin. It had four wheels and was known as a "pleasure wagon." We may assume the name was not descriptive but was given to indicate a vehicle not primarily for freight. The body had no springs at all but, to make riding in it endurable, the seat bounced on two hickory cantilevers. It is easy to guess and impossible to prove that the pleasure wagon was the ancestor of the buggy and of the station wagon.

Wealthy town-dwellers imported sedan chairs and coaches, chariots and phaetons. John Winthrop had the first sedan chair in 1646; Ben Franklin still used one in 1789. In the years between, the elegant were carried through the towns in them, sometimes with Indians as bearers. In time it was possible to use horse-drawn equipages for journeys, if the passengers had sufficient hardihood. Widening a mile of Indian trail to the minimum width for vehicles required clearing nearly a quarter of an acre of land, and people had other clearing to do that they felt was more profitable. What progress was made came from the system of allowing people to "work off" their taxes on the roads. "Clearing" meant cutting trees. Such things as boulders, stumps, and mud holes were left as they stood. A coach driver always carried an ax to clear obstructions and his male passengers were called upon to push when necessary.

A covered bridge

Bridges and Ferries

Naturally, the roads that fanned out into the country from each town were improved somewhat as they were increasingly used, and bridges began to be built. The first bridges crossed only narrow streams and were made of three or four logs, thrown from bank to bank, with smaller logs or planks laid athwart them. When these structures sagged, almost of their own weight, they were stiffened with trusses built above the outside "girders."

By building a couple of stone piers and connecting them with short trussed bridges, wider streams could be crossed. But weather rotted the trusses, so, unless the whole wooden structure was replaced by stone arches, each truss was sheathed with planks to protect it. Gradually the trusses were increased in height to carry longer spans. Then the whole bridge was roofed over and the sides were enclosed. Before they finished with covered bridges, some were more than a mile long.

At most places where a road crossed a wide river, some local man added a bit to his income by operating a flatboat ferry. This was a shallow scow, long enough to carry a wagon and at least

A trussed bridge and a pleasure wagon

four horses. A rope stretched across the river and, running through a couple of pulleys on the upstream side of the boat, overcame the effort of the current to carry the ferry down with it. The stream could even be made to help the boat across by shortening the hitch of the forward pulley. On deep rivers the ferrymen rowed with long sweeps, but ordinarily they set poles against the bottom and walked from bow to stern. Progress was slow.

A flatboat ferry.
The vehicle is a gig

A postrider

The Post and the News

Something of the hit-or-miss handling of mail has been mentioned. It continued nearly to the end of the seventeenth century; then, while the roads were still trails, an official overland postal service was set up. It improved very slowly with the roads. By 1717 a letter from Boston to Williamsburg took four weeks in the summertime; in winter it took twice as long. Benjamin Franklin and William Hunter were made joint Postmasters General for the Colonies in 1753 and mail began to move. Postriders were organized in shifts, so that letters went forward by night as well as by day.

The postrider traveled on horseback, of course, carrying his mail in a couple of saddlebags. At first he went only so far and so fast as his horse's strength would allow and laid over until the next day, or the day after that if the weather was bad. Franklin and Hunter made arrangements for him to change horses at fixed points and keep going on something like a schedule. The rider picked up a little extra change by executing private jobs along the road; in fact, there is a record of one rider delivering a span of oxen for a client. It was the postrider's duty to collect money for his mail, for postage was paid then by the receiver of a letter not by its sender. There's something to be said for the

system: quite a lot of modern mail would go undelivered if the addressee had to pay for it!

Every town had its crier who read out proclamations at the top of his lungs. His news was official only; it lacked interest and detail that could best be given in print. The first American newspaper was the *Boston News Letter,* issued in 1704. John Campbell, its publisher, was the town postmaster. He took advantage of his position to distribute his sheet. Actually it was a public service and the postmasters of other towns came to do the same thing. Franklin did it in Philadelphia but, when he became Postmaster General, he ordered all postriders to carry *all* newspapers; and when Massachusetts read what Virginia was thinking, freedom took a long stride forward.

Inns

Even on horseback it wasn't possible to travel very far in a day over Colonial roads; in a coach, progress was still slower. As late as 1765, travelers had to stop three nights on the road from New York to Boston. A good profit could be made by providing for their needs, so inns and ordinaries appeared at obvious stopping points, just as motor courts do now.

The eighteenth-century ordinaries were more truly public houses than their predecessors had been. They might be described, in modern terms, as combination "diners" and "tourist homes." They catered to wagoners and to simple travelers, who expected to eat what they were given, but the great were not above being entertained in an ordinary when darkness and exhaustion demanded it.

The better inns were located at crossroads and ferries, and the still better ones, where a guest might live for days or weeks, while attending court or waiting for a ship to sail, were in the towns. Some of these were good to the point of luxury; there was the "Green Dragon" in Boston, the "Black Horse" in New York, the "George" in Philadelphia, the "Blue Bell" in Annapolis, and the "Raleigh" in Williamsburg. Treasonous discussions were held in all of them and, in the days preceding the crisis, many were used for indignation meetings. The best tavern in all the Colonies was the "Sun," run by the good Moravians, at Bethlehem, Pennsylvania. A model of cleanliness

A family coach leaving a Southern ordinary

and comfort, it went so far as to provide a personal servant for each of its more distinguished guests.

River Boats

The easiest way to travel and to transport goods was still by water. The Southern planters maintained long "barges," provided with awninged seats in the stern, and rowed by four, six, or even eight slaves. These they used for local visiting and

for church-going. The Northerners were less luxurious about it, but they made full use of the waterways. A church was built on Manhattan Island with its main entrance facing the Hudson for the convenience of parishioners arriving in boats.

It was easy, and reasonably quick, to float produce down the rivers from the back country, and there were many rivers, so nearly every section had its version of the "fall boat." Many were

Fall boats

An early schooner and a cargo ship

thrown together, to be abandoned at the river's mouth, but some were sturdier vessels, intended to be reloaded at tidewater and brought back upstream by laborious rowing or poling or both. The New England "gundalow" had a mast and a lateen sail like that of a Nile river boat. These gundalows and the Durham boats on the Delaware were of the permanent kind.

Ships

Longer journeys were made in ships, including, of course, trips to England, where a good many people went. The trip from Boston to London required a minimum of twenty-six days and from all ports farther south the time was longer. There was little visiting for pleasure between Colony and Colony. You went only if you had to go, because the trip was, at best, arduous and dangerous.

But if you did go, you sailed in an American-built vessel. The magnificent timber in this country was made to order for an age of wooden ships, and there were shipyards in every seaport. Many ships were built for American merchants, but great numbers were commissioned for English owners, who jumped at the chance of buying a sound craft for about a third of what it would cost in Europe. There came a time when a large proportion of all English tonnage was built here.

The hulls of the larger vessels followed the British pattern, regardless of the kind and number of their sails. They were quite tubby in shape, and they clung to modifications of the bulky stern gallery and quarter galleries of the preceding century, and also to the hornlike "head" that projected from the bow. However, the Americans broke away from tradition in their smaller craft, built for fishing and for coastwise trade. They used fewer square sails, hung crosswise, and more of the handy fore-and-aft sails, hung parallel to the keel. They began to experiment with faster hull shapes, too. New England produced the schooner, now found wherever sailboats are used. The Chesapeake Bay shipwrights slowly developed the sharp narrow hull of the Baltimore clipper, the fastest thing afloat.

Rope

Wherever there were ships there had to be rope, and rope, in the eighteenth century, had to be twisted by hand. The work was done in extremely long sheds known as ropewalks; many were as long as three city blocks. Nearly all rope was made of hemp grown on American farms, and the process of making it, though it looked different, was really much like spinning yarn. In fact, the product of the first step was called yarn.

124

Laying a rope

A "head" of hackled hemp was wrapped around the spinner's waist, and a loose end was made fast to a hook belted to the big "spinning wheel." As the wheel was turned by an assistant, the spinner moved backward down the ropewalk, feeding material from his waist and controlling the "draw," just as his wife did at her wheel at home. Working the same way, two or sometimes three yarns were "formed" into a strand. Then three or more strands were "laid" into a rope. To make very heavy cables, or hawsers, such as were attached to anchors, three or more ropes were laid together. At each of these steps the direction of the twist was reversed, thus the parts worked against one another and kept the rope from untwisting. Modern machine-laid rope is still built up on the same principle.

Trade and Money

Many American merchants, especially north of Philadelphia, used their ships to make fortunes for themselves. Whaling was one way. When Britain relaxed restrictions on who might traffic in slaves, the Yankees, particularly the Rhode Islanders, promptly went into the business and evolved the ingenious triangular trade. They made rum and sold it in Africa, buying slaves there to be sold in Cuba, to buy molasses for making rum at home— and they paid no income taxes!

Obviously other trade channels were created by

Spinning hemp yarn

American products, and American needs and men took advantage of them. The great obstacle to business was the shortage of hard coin. The theory of mercantilism, which was behind England's colonial policy, demanded an accumulation of gold in the national treasury—in London. To get hold of some cash they could keep, American merchants dealt with any country but England, even if doing so was illegal, as it usually was. The law saw it as outright smuggling, but it was universally practiced by the most upright men in the Colonies, and their fellow townsmen knew all about it and applauded it.

The tolerant attitude extended even to trading

125

with known pirates, who frequently brought their "hot" goods into New York harbor and were openly entertained by the town merchants. Piracy, though a hanging offense, was looked upon by the public much as was rum-running in the 1920's. And, after all, in the 1720's, a man could be hanged for stealing sixpence. The pirates didn't think of themselves as criminals either; they were businessmen.

All this lawless trading *did* bring needed cash into the Colonies. Mostly it was in the form of Spanish or Dutch silver dollars, "pieces of eight." So many of them circulated that, when independence had been won, Congress simply legalized them and made the dollar the basis of American currency.

A silver mug made in America

Silverware

When Colonials got hold of these foreign dollars they tended to hoard them, if only to try to force England to accept commodities as payment. Since all coins had the value of their actual weight (sometimes reduced a bit by judicious "clipping"), a favorite way of keeping them was to have them converted into silverware, "plate," as it was called. The conversion was perfectly legal, even with English money, and in utensil form the silver could be displayed and could be identified if it were stolen.

As a result of the conversion of coin, and of the desire to own handsome plate that came with increasing prosperity, silversmiths hammered away in all the principal centers, but chiefly in the North. The Southerners had only tobacco, and that could be most readily converted into silver in London. Though Colonial silversmiths followed the fashions of England, they followed them in their own way, and their work had a clean vigor that made it as good as any in the world. The best of it has never been equaled since.

Town pump

Towns

Silversmiths and other specialists naturally congregated in towns, where life had taken a turn toward luxury and ostentation. By the mid-eighteenth century Philadelphia had become one of the principal English cities of the world. It had brick-paved streets and a flourishing commerce. Boston and Salem grew rich on fish and trade. New York was a local center, not due to equal Philadelphia until after the Erie Canal was finished in 1825. Annapolis, Williamsburg, and Charleston were local centers, too, distinguished more for their sophistication and intellectual attainments than for their trade, though there was no lack of wealth in any of them. The first two came to life only twice a year, while the Assemblies were in session; they slept contentedly through the months between.

126

Buildings

Virginia was the richest of the Colonies, so, when she moved her capital to Williamsburg in 1699, she could afford to put up buildings that were prime examples of the latest taste. The town already boasted a structure to challenge the best efforts of anybody, the College of William and Mary, almost certainly from the drafting board of Christopher Wren himself, the man who started the style we now call Georgian.

Most of the Englishmen who tried to follow Wren muffed the attempt but one of them, James Gibbs, caught his spirit and, in 1728, produced an illustrated *Book of Architecture*. With Gibbs's book in one hand, American "undertakers" (contractors) waded into creating Georgian buildings. Fortunately these men had never seen the tame English copies of Wren, and they had the inborn good taste that was mysteriously universal at the time. For it wasn't only in Williamsburg that handsome buildings were put up: the Wren influence, and the fine proportions that belong with it, can be found from South Carolina to Maine.

Often a builder worked with no other plans than an architectural book (Gibbs's was the first of many) and such drawings as he might scratch on a board with an awl when the need arose. Some of these boards have been found, built into the houses they described. That the architectural books were used is certain, because large sections of houses and churches can be matched to plates in the books.

It was fashionable for gentlemen to be amateurs of architecture, and some were notably proficient. The great Philadelphia lawyer, Andrew Hamilton, tossed off Independence Hall between briefs. Boston's first Georgian building, the Old North Church, was designed by William Price, a dealer in engravings. Peter Harrison, a Rhode Island merchant and, later, Thomas Jefferson, a lawyer and author, were distinguished architects. These last two belong to the so-called Later Georgian period, which strove so hard to be classical that it sometimes lost sight of the fact that buildings are primarily for human use.

In the seventeenth century the outside appearance of a house was largely the result of the comfortable arrangement of its rooms. The front door was put at the most convenient point for entering the place, the windows wherever light was needed. A Georgian house *had* to have its entrance in the middle, and the same number of windows *had* to be exactly balanced on either side of the door; if it had a wing on one side, it was supposed to have a duplicate wing on the other. All houses of any pretension were now two rooms deep, and the rooms were arranged as best they could be within the symmetrical exterior. In general this resulted in a central hall with two rooms on each side of it.

By far the greater number of Georgian houses were built of brick, with wooden trim painted white, but some in New England, and a few elsewhere, had painted wooden walls. In Pennsylvania cut stone was always preferred to either brick or wood. The general shape was similar everywhere, a rectangular block topped by a "hipped" roof, sloping upward from all four walls. Some, like the one illustrated, had gambrel roofs to give headroom inside. Roofs were quite steep before 1750; after that they were made lower, to conform with the proportions of a classic temple roof.

Wooden framing, inside the walls, continued to be made of heavy timbers, secured with mortise-and-tenon joints. The modern "balloon" frame, of small timbers nailed together, was invented in Chicago many years later, when houses were needed in a hurry. As a general thing, eighteenth-century chimneys were kept near the middle of a house in the North, and at the ends in the South, as they had been for nearly a century. The chimneys of Mt. Vernon were originally at the ends, but General Washington built out beyond them.

Small houses copied the large ones in a simplified way that was exactly right. In addition to their excellent over-all proportions, one of the things that makes these houses, both big and little, attractive is the smallness of their windows. The eye is rested on the pleasant expanses of wall between them. This may be an argument against modern copies, for windows of original size leave them too dark for modern taste and with larger windows their nice proportions are lost.

The wealthy of this time made a cult of elegant living, but they took for granted crudities that would be tolerated only by the lowest of modern standards. There was, for instance, but one house in all the Colonies with an inside bathroom—and it was strictly for bathing. There was only one house (not the same one) with running water, piped from a spring to the kitchen only. A few people had outside bathhouses, enclosing a small stone "tub" into which water could be poured from buckets and warmed by dropping in heated stones. Almost everybody did his "bathing" in his bedroom from a basin and didn't do enough of it to endanger his health. Hot water for bathing and shaving was brought from the kitchen by a servant. All houses had at least one outdoor privy, called, with dubious euphemism, the House of Necessity. Mansions usually had two of them, exact duplicates, built as ornamental features of the garden. Among the aristocratic, these were used only by the young men and by white servants. Ladies and older men had commodes in their bedchambers which were cared for by servants.

Rooms

The formal, elaborately framed front door of a mansion was often topped by a carved pineapple, sometimes painted in natural colors; it was a symbol of hospitality. Real pineapples were rare curiosities raised in greenhouses from ratoons that had survived weeks on shipboard. Beyond the door a visitor entered a wide reception hall from which rose an imposing staircase, reaching the second floor at an easy angle and usually broken by one or two landings. Sometimes one landing was over the front door. At first, the ends of the steps were covered by a stringpiece that followed the slope of the stair and on which the balusters were set; later, the step ends were exposed and carved and the balusters were set directly on the treads. Most balusters were turned and sometimes carved as well, even to the point of having three quite different ones on each step; but by the time that was done, the Americans were beginning to think about oiling their muskets against the redcoats.

In the first quarter of the century, all downstairs rooms in most houses were paneled. A series of moldings formed a cornice where the woodwork met the ceiling, and a projecting chair rail ran all the way around the room at about the height of the window sills. Thick walls made deep window recesses that were faced with small panels. These were usually hinged next to the window and were actually inside shutters.

All of the woodwork was painted, as a rule, and in one flat color that was no "pastel shade." The colors were seldom brilliant, but they were good strong gray blues, olive greens, dark reds, and ochers. At first there were no mantel shelves: the

A Maryland stairhall

paneling was finished off around the fireplaces with a heavy frame of moldings, painted like the rest of the room.

After 1750 "paper hangings," that is to say, wallpaper, became popular and plaster walls were provided for it above the chair rail. Below the rail the panels remained, as a dado. When the wall was plaster, the cornice often was also, being "run" in place by a skilled workman and an apprentice assistant. The helper provided a continuous supply of mixed material and the master pushed a cutout metal form around the wall, shaping the cornice, complete, behind him. Perhaps this skill could be revived if it were needed, but there are few, if any, who can practice it at the present writing.

Colonial wallpaper didn't come in rolls; it came in smallish sheets, limited by the size of the papermaker's mold. The designs were hand-printed from engraved wooden blocks. Only one color was printed; the rest were stenciled on or painted freehand. Often a whole series of sheets were painted to be assembled into a romantic scene, or a scattered assemblage of birds and flowers, with no reiterated pattern.

Floors were now made of boards four or five inches wide instead of extremely wide ones. In the North, floors were often decorated with a border, stenciled on with paint; sometimes there was also a stenciled medallion in the center of the room. "Carpets" had come off the tables to lie on the floor as we are used to seeing them. Ordinary households made their own rugs by braiding or weaving hoarded rags, but the wealthy imported costly Orientals, or rugs made entirely of the cross-stitched needlework known as *gros point*. To some eyes, these are the most beautiful floor coverings ever devised. There were also "floor cloths," of linen canvas or coarsely woven wool, that were painted with stencils. In summer, especially in the South, people put their rugs away and covered the floors with straw matting.

A chest-on-chest

A highboy

Furniture

Much furniture was imported, but demand created supply and increasing amounts were made in the Colonies, especially in Pennsylvania and Rhode Island. Almost all fine furniture for the first fifty years of the century was made of walnut; after that, most of it was mahogany. The style of Thomas Chippendale dominated the later years, after the publication of his book, *The Gentleman and Cabinet-Maker's Director,* in 1754.

There were numerous earlier assists from England. The fashions of the reigns of William and Mary and of Anne influenced the shapes of American furniture, as it expanded from the basic necessities used in the seventeenth century. A chest was first given drawers to make it more convenient; then it was set on short legs to make the drawers easier to reach. It was then a "chest of drawers." To save space, one chest of drawers was set upon another, to make what is called a "chest-on-chest." Put longer legs under the two chests and you had a "highboy." The "lowboy" is said to have resulted from the use of a highboy base without the top section.

Tables were made in great variety. The old gate-leg had various descendants with drop leaves that sometimes reached almost to the floor. Three tables of this kind, made to match, could be put

A lowboy

A wing chair and a tilt-top table

together to form a banquet board eighteen feet long, or even longer. Card tables were known as "gaming tables" and were made with circular projections at each corner to hold candlesticks; many of them had also small depressions hollowed in their tops to hold money. There were many tea tables, some of them made with "pie crust" tops; in these, the surface of the table top was lowered, leaving a raised rim around the edge, which sometimes was scalloped. The tops of these tables were hinged, so they could be tilted and stood against a wall.

Bed wrench

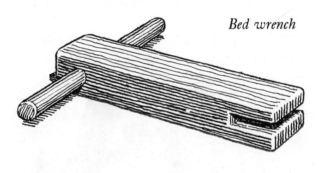

Although this slight account is omitting hosts of articles, some mention must be made of upholstered chairs and of beds. Chairs were upholstered, though never with loose cushions. They were covered with silk damasks and fine brocades, with tapestry, and with the kind of wool embroidery that is called crewelwork, but they weren't really comfortable in the modern sense. People sat erect on chairs then and never lolled on their spines.

Most beds had high posts supporting a canopy called a tester. They had, at the least, token cur-

tains, some of which could actually be drawn to surround the sleeper. Beds were still short and it was still customary to sleep in them reclining on a pile of pillows. The mattress was a feather bed, or a ticking filled with straw or cornhusks; these last were notoriously lumpy. There was no spring. Its place was taken by a rope, laced back and forth across the frame of the bed, a continuous strand that could be tightened, when it sagged, with a wooden bed wrench.

Despite all the superb productions of Colonial cabinetmakers, it's possible that America's greatest furniture-making achievement is what it did with the Windsor chair. The first of these is said to have been found by King George the First in a tavern at Windsor, in England. It was a stiff, clumsy thing, but the King's admiration assured its being copied. When copies reached America, the design underwent a gradual transformation made possible by American hickory and controlled by a taste that had somehow lost the British conviction that strength means weight. The Windsor became light and strong; it yielded slightly to the pressure of the back; the seat tilted back just enough for dignified relaxation. By using wedges at some points, and by inserting dry wood into green, so that shrinkage would grip the inserted piece, the Windsor chair was put together without nails or screws; and it stayed together. Many a one, made almost two hundred years ago, is still in service. The American versions of the chair came in many sizes and varieties, nearly all of them good to look at. They filled a need in the houses of the great and the lowly alike.

Windsor chairs.
The hoop-back is from Pennsylvania,
the comb-back from Massachusetts

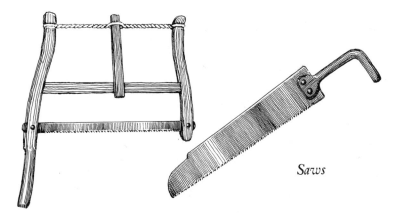

Saws

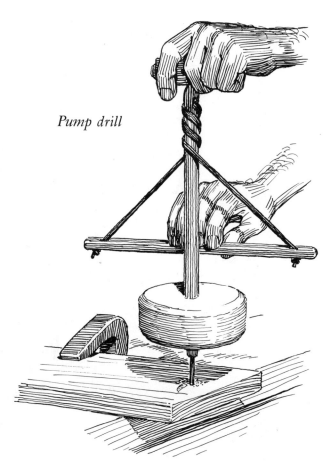

Pump drill

Tools

The eighteenth-century cabinetmaker had all the tools his predecessor, the joiner, had used, and some of them had been improved. He still used saws with narrow blades, stretched in a frame like a bucksaw, but he also had a wide-bladed, open-handled saw that was the ancestor of the modern crosscut saw.

His twist drills were known in the seventeenth century, and long before that, but the later ones have survived and it's better to deal with those, of which there is precise knowledge. There were two kinds. One was the pump drill, which took its spin from the forcible unwinding of two leather thongs from a shaft, and had a kind of flywheel to wind them up again. The other was the bow drill (the ancient Egyptians used it). A bowstring was given one turn around a wooden pulley, of which the drill bit was the fixed axle. Drawing the bow back and forth rotated the drill. The shank of the bit extended a couple of inches above the pulley and rotated freely in a loose cap held by the work-

er's left hand. The grooves of drill bits were not then given a spiral twist; they had instead two straight grooves, opposite one another, and would cut turning either way.

The old spring-pole lathe was still used in the eighteenth century, but cabinetmakers successful enough to have an apprentice used the "Great wheel." It was just that, a wooden wheel six feet or more in diameter, with a crank on its axle to exercise the apprentice. A belt from the rim drove

Bow drill

Lathe with a "great wheel"

a small pulley on the lathe, delivering a steady high-speed spin to the work.

Except for such special matters as lathes, carpenters and cabinetmakers used the same tools. Whole books have been written about old woodworking tools, but this can't be one of them. It is not, after all, the tools that do fine work. It is skill, and taste, and infinite care. It is also public appre-

Pennsylvania six-plate stove

ciation. There's no point in making things well for people who don't know good things from bad ones.

Heat and Light

Though winter living had spread from a single room to several, there was no such thing in the Colonies as a comfortably warm house in the modern sense. All fireplaces could do was to create hot areas; even the four daily cartloads of wood it took to supply the twenty-eight fires of one great mansion did little to take the chill off its icy halls. Fireplaces for heating only were small, and they usually had cast-iron "firebacks" set against their rear walls to radiate more heat. Some of these heating fireplaces were astonishingly shallow, mere niches in the wall, but the flues were so cleverly built that "the smoke went up the chimney just the same."

Stoves for heating were introduced by the Pennsylvania Germans. The first ones were rectangular boxes set on legs. They were made of five iron plates, with the front end left open. Later a sixth plate was added, with a door in it that allowed the draft to be controlled. It was

133

A whale-oil lamp and a pistol tinder

the old five-plate heater that gave Benjamin Franklin his idea for an iron fireplace with a baffled air box in it, around which hot gases could be forced to circulate. Air, passing through the box, was delivered to a room hot and smoke-less. The advantage was more even heating, and Franklin stoves became understandably popular in New England within a couple of years after Ben announced them.

Starting a fire was still a difficult problem, and the old tinderbox was to be found in every household, but some improvements had been made and were used by those who could afford them. One was the tinder wheel or tinder mill. It was a solid steel wheel, mounted on one end of an open metal box in which tinder was placed. A string, wrapped on the wheel's axle and pulled smartly, would spin the wheel against a flint and deliver a healthy shower of sparks to the tinder.

The other fire-starter involved the use of a kind of firearm. The flintlock, for firing guns,

Iron snuffers and a brass extinguisher

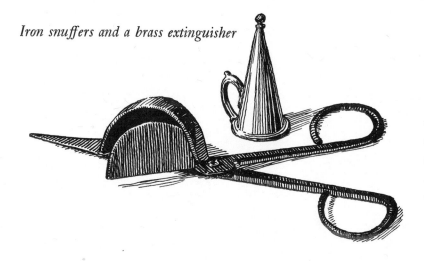

had become quite common by 1700. Someone hit on the idea of adapting it to a fire-lighter and built the "pistol tinder," which was handy but too expensive for most people. It was like a pistol with no barrel, but it had a complete flintlock mechanism. The flashpan was a tinderbox and, in addition to ordinary tinder, a grain or two of powder could be put in as a booster. This would blaze from a spark and light the tinder about four times out of five tries. A pistol tinder had two metal feet on its front end, so that, with the butt making a third foot, it would sit upright on a shelf. It also had a ring on it for a candle-end to catch the light from the tinder.

Two improvements were made in lighting, and the whale provided the means for both of them. One was the spermaceti candle, made from wax obtained from the sperm whale's head. It gave three times the light of a tallow candle and smoked less. The other was the whale-oil lamp.

Sperm whales were hard to catch. So the candles made from their wax were too expensive for the average household, and the cost of lighting a big house, where forty or fifty of them might burn in a single night, was formidable indeed. Such houses commonly had a servant whose whole evening duty was attending to the candles: replacing those that had burned too short or were dripping badly, snuffing the wicks of those that had begun to smoke. Snuffing was shortening the wick by clipping it; the candle was not extinguished. The operation was performed with a pair of special shears, equipped with a small box on one blade to catch the wick ends. Practical snuffers could be made of wrought iron, but those for social use had silver handles and rested on a small silver tray. A metal cone was used to extinguish candles; and they were lighted with a wax taper, ignited at the fire.

When a candle flame blows in the wind, it drips messily and wastefully. Windows weren't weather-stripped in the eighteenth century, and there were always draughts. The high-backed settle and the wing chair attest the fact, so does the hurricane globe, a tall and shapely glass "chimney" large enough to sit on a table and enclose an entire candlestick. Cool air came downward over its edge and warm air was discharged up the middle. Even a stiff breeze wouldn't disturb the flame of a candle in a hurricane globe. There is a hurricane

Petticoat lamp

globe in the illustration of the Maryland stairhall.

Whale oil became reasonably cheap, so that most people could afford to burn it in lamps. The lamp itself was nothing more than a covered cup with a wick that passed through a hole in the lid. There was no chimney of any kind, though the lamps may have been set in hurricane globes on windy nights. Whale-oil lamps were made with varying bases: some sat squat, some stood on pedestals, and one, the petticoat lamp, had a socket base that allowed it to be set on the top knob of a ladder-back chair, to provide light for reading. The ingenious Dr. Franklin made an improvement in this kind of lamp; he gave it two wicks.

Food, Eating, and Cookery

Prosperity and security, as well as the taste of the times, brought about a more expansive and formal way of living in the towns. This affected the prosperous middle class of tradesmen and independent artisans, as well as the rich. A shopkeeper would have a room in his modest house that was set aside for eating and, since such a man always had one or two servants, it was used. The same thing was not true in the country. If a farmhouse had a dining room at all, it was used only on great occasions; the kitchen remained the living center of the house. Naturally, this doesn't apply to country mansions.

A dining room demanded attention to the appearance of the table. Linen damask replaced the older huckaback and dowlas board-cloth and napkins. The napkins of the eighteenth century were nearly as big as a modern card-table cover and were customarily tied around the diner's neck to protect frills and furbelows. Forks appeared around the turn of the century, steel ones, with bone handles and only two tines. They had only the purpose of holding meat down to be cut; to carry food to the mouth on a fork would have been bad manners. But that didn't last long and, by 1750, finger-eating had become taboo among the best people. Silver forks appeared then; they had three tines and were much smaller than a modern dinner fork. With silver forks came dinner knives. They had "pistol" handles, ending in a scroll. There were silver spoons too, of course, made with the tapering "rat tail" on the backs of the bowls.

The big, standing salt went out of fashion and was sent off to the silversmith to be melted and made into individual "trencher" salts, some standing on solid bases and some on three small feet. The empty place in the center of the table left by the banished salt was filled by an elaborate silver *epergne,* when the householder could afford one. It was purely ornamental and consisted of a central dish on a high stand, surrounded by three or four smaller dishes supported on arms attached to the pedestal. Fruit, flowers, or sweetmeats could be put into the dishes. Silver candelabra were put on the table when they were needed; otherwise they stayed on the sideboard.

A few people began to use china plates for eating. They were imported from England and as a rule were plain white "salt glaze" stuff, the glaze being produced by throwing pulverized salt into the kiln at a judicious moment. English potters were experimenting and improving and in time some of their finer wares came to the Colonies.

Silver trencher salt

A potter "throwing" a crock on his wheel

Apparently nothing that could properly be called china or porcelain was made in America; our potters confined themselves to sturdy jugs, bowls, beer pots, and the kind of large crock in which pickles were stored.

The revolving table on which clay is shaped into pots helps the craftsman to keep his work symmetrical. Modern potters' wheels can be rotated by electric motors; the Colonial potter had to keep his own wheel turning. He did it with his feet, by giving an occasional shove to a large and heavy flywheel mounted below his bench. Flywheel and work table were fixed at opposite ends of the same vertical shaft.

Late in the century, when American ships had begun trading with the Orient, people began ordering porcelain from China. This Chinese export stuff somehow came to be miscalled Lowestoft. Real Lowestoft is entirely different. The Chinese would decorate their china to order, and the pieces often sported heraldry that the buyer felt he was entitled to use. One gentleman sent out a careful drawing of his coat of arms on which he marked a hasty, last-minute change, something like "make this red," with an arrow. Back came his dinner service, forever marked with the arms *and* the correction—note, arrow, and all!

Most tableware was pewter throughout the eighteenth century. It, or wood, was preferred on the Western frontier—because it didn't dull a man's knife. Pewter absorbs heat quickly, but it doesn't hold it. This led to plate-warming racks by dining-room fires, and to pewter plates and platters made double, with a space between the top and bottom surfaces to be filled with hot water. The problem of keeping food warm from kitchen to dining room in a spottily heated house was bad, but it was still worse when the dinner went out of doors on its way to the table. Covered dishes were universal and large houses often had serving rooms, with a fire where food could be kept warm or reheated.

The food that went on eighteenth-century tables was pretty much the same as what was eaten in the seventeenth. It was better served, and old dishes were fancified a little, but it ran to things that were smoked, salted, dried, or pickled. There was still no refrigeration good enough to keep fresh meat from spoiling in summer and only in the North, where ice could be cut and stored, covered with sawdust or straw, in roofed pits, was there any refrigeration at all. The best the South could do was the relative coolness of a stone springhouse, where water ran through shallow troughs that were always home to a frog or two. A springhouse would delay the souring of milk.

Corn remained the great staple, in spite of a steady increase in the supply of wheat flour, which came into general use but was reserved in most households for special occasions. An illustration of this is found in the "grace" with which a country swain embarrassed his girl when his town-bred rival stayed for Sunday supper:

> The Lord be praised. I am amazed
>   To see how things are mended.
> Shortcake and tea for supper I see,
>   When mush and milk was intended!

Springhouse

By and large, the North ate yellow meal, the South, white. The yellow was coarser ground. Of it, the dry, thin johnnycake was made. Also from the yellow meal was made the famous "Indian pudding" that, after baking eighteen hours in a brick oven, had the consistency of stiff jelly when it was turned out on a platter. Southern spoon bread, or corn pone, was the best product of the white meal. It, too, was cooked slowly and long, until it enclosed its own soft innards in a thick brown crust. It was (and, thank Heaven, is) served hot.

A list of common foods for the seventeenth century will do for the eighteenth. Game was still so plentiful that it was for sale in all urban markets at all seasons. Bear bacon was common in the Alleghenies, but rare in the East. Old smoked ham belonged to the East, especially to the Southeast. After hanging in a smokehouse for several years a ham acquired fine flavor and became so hard it would almost ring when it was hit. But after it had been soaked two days and simmered for five or six hours, it was surpassingly good food. Virginians preferred it cold—for breakfast.

The rich imported luxuries, but they had to be durable luxuries. We know of coffee and tea, of "cocoa nuts" (chocolate), of olives, almonds, raisins, and lemons. Not having tasted these things, the poor man hardly missed them. He had molasses, honey, maple sugar, apple butter, sweet pickles, or preserved watermelon rind, depending on where he lived. He had loaf sugar, too; a lot of it was smuggled in. Spices were looked upon almost as a necessity. Even those who prided themselves on self-sufficiency bought salt, sugar, and spice. The rich man had his Madeira and Canary wines; the poor man was content with beer and cider, with a little rum for holidays.

Meat pies have an origin too old to be accounted for. What we call mince pie was a meat pie originally, but the dried fruits in it gradually came to dominate the meat, which has dwindled to a token bit of suet. Fresh fruit pies, baked in a crust like meat pies, are an American invention that has never become popular elsewhere. Our first pies weren't round. They were baked in rectangular pans and were known as "trap" pies if they had no top crust, or, if they had one, as "coffin" pies. Today's good cook prides herself on the tenderness of her crust; not so her forebears. The crusts of pies that were to be kept were made deliberately stiff and tough, though how a pie crust could be a help in preservation isn't now clear. By mixing rye flour with hot water, a really notable toughness could be achieved. Wheat flour and mutton broth, as a pie-crust "receipt," isn't looked upon with favor by modern cooks, either.

The crust of brick-oven bread was thick and hard, too. Children often tried to hide it in their clothing, or feed it to the dog, to avoid eating it. Many people cut bread crusts off and saved them to be stewed in milk as "brewis." This mush was eaten as porridge, or poured over meat as a thick gravy.

The kitchen went on much as it had in the previous century. Stoves were for heat. Their introduction had no effect on cooking methods. The open hearth and the brick oven continued in universal use. In the fireplace, the wooden lug pole was gone, except in the backwoods. In its place was an iron "back pole" or a crane. A pot could be hung on a crane without risking incineration. All ovens were now built with their doors facing the kitchen instead of opening into the fireplace. This too helped to avoid scorching the cook. Some utensils were improved, and some gadgets were added. A hollowed-out stone sink gave the cook a place to wash vegetables and an easy way to get rid of waste water, though it was discharged just beyond the kitchen wall and lay on the ground in a puddle to delight the ducks.

Perhaps the "roasting kitchen" was invented at the latter end of the previous century, but the

A clock jack and a roasting kitchen

The mechanism of a smoke jack

spected and basted. That was another advantage of the rig: it was easier to catch drippings in it than in an open pan on the hearth; also, it was easier on the cook, the meat didn't have to be as close to the heat as it did on an ordinary spit.

A roasting kitchen couldn't handle a very large roast, so spits were still extensively used, and various mechanisms were introduced for turning them. Some of these were "jacks," so called because they were substitutes for spit-turning boys, who were sometimes hard to capture when needed. Clock jacks were turned by wound-up springs, and rotated the meat vertically, like the old twisted cords. Smoke jacks worked in the chimney, where the rising column of hot air rotated their windmill-like vanes. The rotation was transferred to the spit by a chain drive.

Barring a captive boy, the most successful way to rotate the roast was by the efforts of a turnspit dog. The breed is all but extinct. They are good-natured and short-legged terriers, and they used to be trained to walk in a cylindrical cage or on a treadmill. In either case, they generated enough power to justify their name. The turnspit learned to do the job patiently, but never to like it; and he developed an uncanny knack for knowing just when to be elsewhere, like the boy he replaced. A generation that accepted human slavery as a natural thing made nothing of enslaving a canine. Larger dogs were trained for similar work, evidently. Churning was often a dog job, and the treadmills for the purpose are far too heavy to be operated by a little turnspit terrier.

known ones all date from the eighteenth or later. It was a metal box with one open side that faced the fire. The box stood on legs, and a spit, turned by a crank on the outside, ran through it from end to end. Roasting kitchens had doors in their backs through which the cooking meat could be in-

Turnspits and their treadmill.
A rail that usually enclosed the working dog has been omitted for clarity

Rotary broiler, warming shelf, teakettle, and toaster

The fancier cookery of more sophisticated living modified some standard cooking utensils and fathered some new ones. An iron pot grew a spout and became a teakettle. Tea became very popular in the Colonies during the first half of the eighteenth century, though it has never recovered from the blow it received in Boston harbor in 1773.

An iron shelf for warming serving dishes was made to hang on a bar placed across the andirons. A wrought-iron toaster swung on a pin at the end of its long handle, so that the toast could be "done" on both sides without being touched. A broiler had a rotating top; all of the meat on it could be cooked evenly by giving each part its turn near the fire.

The dating of kitchen utensils is almost impossible; the best one can do is to assume that the more elaborate ones are the later. A wooden rolling pin with two rollers was probably made after a single one. A wooden potato masher with a turned handle is obviously more sophisticated than one with a whittled handle. The use of copper in the kitchen increased with time. A copper strainer shaped like a porringer suggests that somebody made the first one by punching holes in the bottom of an actual porringer. There were wooden strainers, too, and neat funnels turned out of maple.

Eggs were beaten and cream was whipped. Either job could be done with an improvised whisk, but it was slow work. Yankee ingenuity was equal to the problem. A wooden beater that could be rotated between the palms of the hands was made. Some carpenter took a look at the thing,

and at his own bow drill, and combined the two into the bow beater, which would do the job as well as anything not equipped with a motor. Such a gimmick was not "merchandised" as it might be now; it was merely copied by anyone who liked it. So its use spread slowly, and no two examples were exactly alike.

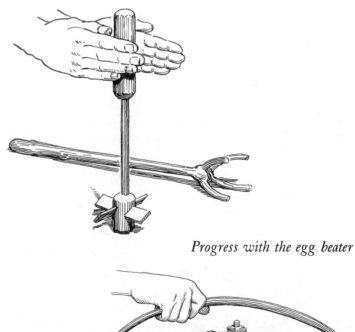

Progress with the egg beater

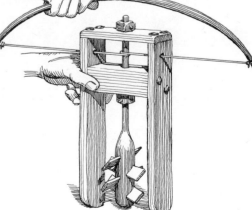

Fop at mid-century

Men's Clothes

A debonair detachment of manner was thought necessary by a mid-eighteenth-century dandy. His clothes were as rich as his purse would permit, his gestures were as studied as any actor's, and his speech bristled with the latest eccentric oaths, used regardless of sense or meaning: "Strike me blue!" "Stab my vitals!" He flourished the lace at his cuff as daintily he took snuff from a golden box, and as daintily sneezed. But this was no "lily." He was an accomplished horseman and swordsman and, though he thought it beneath a gentleman to *aim* a pistol, he would happily let one off in your general direction if you offended his tetchy honor. He would, of course, allow you to reciprocate at the same time.

The extreme clothes of the London beau were modified on this side of the water, especially on the backs of the soberer worthies, but they had their influence. Judges, merchants, and landowners sported velvets and satins in glowing colors. It goes without saying that men who worked with their hands didn't wear lace at their wrists, nor did gentlemen when riding upon journeys or on common occasions in the country; but any gentleman dressed for church, or for business in town, wore it. The lace was attached to the sleeve of a "lawn" shirt that, alas, was not invariably immaculate.

The amount of lace worn at a man's wrists varied with fashion from a narrow frill to a cascade that covered his hands. Lace bands (collars) had been worn in the 1660's but the lace falls at the throat that seem to belong with wigs and silver buckles didn't get started until after 1725. In the early years of the century, a plain strip of white linen was tied around the neck, its two broad ends spreading on the breastbone. It was called a gorget. To this everyday fashion the Steenkirk was shortly added. It was a long silk scarf, black or white, wrapped twice around the neck and hitched, like a stock. The ends were allowed to hang loose, outside the waistcoat. In George the Second's time, the Steenkirk, or something quite like it, was tied in a pussycat bow and the first of the lace falls flowed from under it. A restrained example appears in the illustration at the head of this section. The bow didn't last long. It was replaced by a linen neckband, to which the fall was attached, sometimes with a jeweled pin or a buckle. Few wore lace every day; most people couldn't afford it, and there were always conservatives who wouldn't wear it under any circumstances. The plain linen neckcloth, worn

Steenkirk scarf

throughout the eighteenth century by unpretentious men, was actually a short Steenkirk.

To trace the changes rung upon men's coats in the eighteenth century would take half of this book. Some of the minor variations appear incidentally in the illustrations. Here, we can mention four versions: As it began in the reign of William and Mary, hanging loose from the shoulders, with stiffened, buttoned-back cuffs that reached to the elbow; pinch-waisted and short-tailed, about 1725; swinging wide again, with stiffened skirts, at mid-century, and again with big cuffs, but limp this time; and last, calming down to the decent, long coat with a moderate cuff, or none, that we are used to seeing in the pictures of the Founding Fathers.

The name "waistcoat," applied to the sleeveless garment that was universally worn under a coat, usually didn't describe it very well. Not until the battles of the Revolution were over did the waistcoat permanently get up as high as the waist—in front at least. Usually it was a couple of inches shorter than the coat itself and was little more than an apron, with skirts in front and the same kind of back that a vest now has. The early waistcoats were complete garments, sleeveless but skirted all the way around. House servants continued to wear this kind, with no coat, when they were going about their chores, though they wore coats over them in public.

A gentleman's waistcoat on any festive occasion might, like his coat, be of velvet or satin, and it was frequently ornamented with embroidered flowers in glowing colors. Plainer ones were naturally used for daily wear and practical people wore cloth coats with waistcoats to match.

Breeches sometimes matched the outfit, but more often they were darker or lighter than the upper garments. Breeches didn't have the modern fly front. A band buttoned around the waist and a square, flap front was buttoned up to it, with six or eight buttons. The arrangement survived until recently on the "bell-bottomed trousers" of U. S. sailors. Full breeches disappeared entirely and were never seen again until the bicycle was invented. Instead, "small clothes" were so tight that they had to be split at the knee and buttoned, as riding breeches still are. Until the middle of the century, and even after, stockings were pulled up

Breeches

over the breeches and were held by an exposed garter, just below or just above the knee.

From using no buttons at all, Colonial men came to use an excess of them. They appeared on cuffs and pockets, and on the backs of coats, as well as in long rows down the full length of coat and waistcoat. Nobody ever buttoned all of them. Most buttons were metal and were ornamented in some way. They had crests and flowers on them, in relief, or they were enameled, or even jeweled. Silver and gold and brass were extensively used for buttons. Even unpretentious people needed a great many. They couldn't afford the handsome ones, so they cast their own from pewter in wooden molds, exactly as they cast bullets.

A button mold and its product

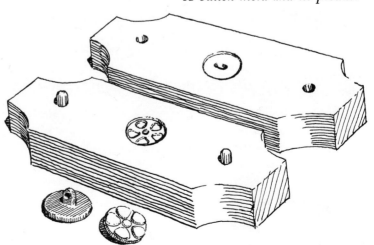

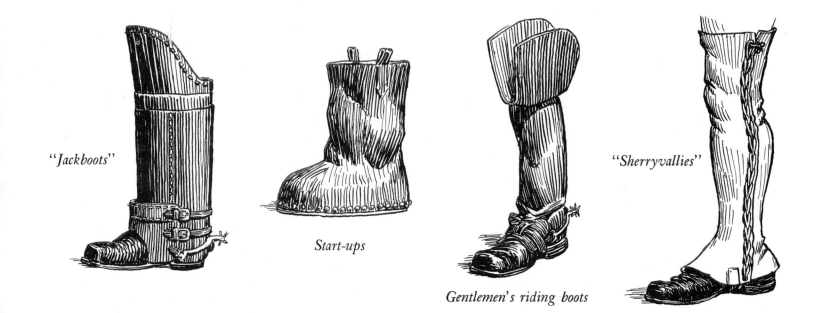

"Jackboots"

Start-ups

Gentlemen's riding boots

"Sherryvallies"

Most shoes were square-toed, and all were interchangeable between the feet. Men's heels generally were a bit higher than they are now, and some were very high indeed. Up to 1750 a gentleman's heels were more often red than not. Fashion controlled the height of the heel and the length and shape of the shoe tongue. Sometimes the tongue was wide and rounded, sometimes it was long and narrow, standing high above the shoe buckle. Buckles became universal on the shoes of all ages and of both sexes. The poor wore pewter and brass buckles. The rich wore silver and gold and cut-steel, and even jeweled buckles for dressy events.

Mud was a constantly recurring Colonial fact. Men didn't wear pattens in muddy weather as women did; many of them wore clogs; but town dwellers, above the laboring class, usually put on golo-shoes, start-ups, or buskins. All three were clumsy things that went over regular shoes; they had heavy soles, usually wooden, with leather or canvas tops. Buskins were tied to the leg just below the knee. Start-ups reached the calf and made shift to stand alone. Golo-shoes were ankle-high.

"Jackboots," for riding, were made of boiled leather and were so thick and stiff that the legs of them had to be wide, in order to get the feet in. Nobody did any walking in jackboots that he didn't have to do. Lighter leather leggings or gaiters, called "sherryvallies," were also worn for riding. They reached the thigh and had "feet" like modern spats, with a strap under the arch of the foot to keep them from slipping up the leg. These leggings were buckled with short straps up the sides, or secured by the same kind of interlocking loops that fastened the doublets of the first settlers.

Unless he was wearing a cap, for working, the inevitable topping of every man's outfit was a cocked hat, or what had been one; sometimes they became pretty limp from wetting and lack of care.

Basic wig styles

Periwig

Grizzle wig

Campaign wig

Ramillies wig

The cocked hat went through just about every conceivable shape before it settled down to its classic three-cornered form. Hats were nearly always black, but they weren't all plain; they were often decorated with gold braid, or edged with feathers or fur, this almost up to the time of the Stamp Act.

Wigs remained in style through this whole century and were worn even beyond it by elderly conservatives: Wigs were considered as essential as breeches. Any gentleman whose wig was knocked off was deeply embarrassed. This is understandable, because heads were shaved for comfort and the most hair any man wore under his wig was what we now would call a short crew cut. Farmers, "mechanicks," and artisans didn't wear wigs as a rule, but almost everybody else did; they were worn by children, servants, soldiers, even convicts, sometimes at third or fourth hand or, rather, head.

The full periwig clung on until about 1725, along with wigs of other shapes, notably the "Ramillies" that had a puff surrounding the face and a long braided tail or two hanging down behind. The suffocating business of powdering wigs began while Queen Anne was still alive, about 1710. One had to put a sheet over his shoulders and then stick his face into a paper cone to avoid choking while the operation was performed. There were stands for wigs, but apparently the powdering had to be done at the last moment, on the owner's head. When a powdered wig was worn outdoors, every breath of air dispersed a little cloud that snowed upon the coat.

Wigs were made of various materials and priced accordingly. Human hair was the most expensive and might cost the equivalent of $250. Cheaper ones were made of horsehair, goathair, calves'

Powdering

tails; silk, linen, and cotton thread; and even of fine wire! The last kind didn't need to be sent out every week to the hairdresser to be cleaned and curled. The curling of wigs was done on small heated rollers of pipe clay, called "buckles," and a wig in process of being curled was said to be "in buckle." Some hairdressers rolled the hair cold and baked the whole wig in an oven, where it often scorched. The cost of maintaining a wig could run to a hundred dollars a year.

Not all wigs were white. Some people favored flaxen ones, or brown, or black. "Grizzle" (gray) wigs were worn by dignified elders and clergymen.

Bob wig

Brown tie wig

Bag wig

Wigless at home

At first they had a shape of their own; later they were likely to be of the "bob" shape favored by Dr. Samuel Johnson. Wigs came in many styles, some highly antic, but most of them approached the shape of natural long hair "clubbed," that is, drawn back and tied. This was the way the "common people" wore their own hair, unpowdered. Wigs were tied, too, not always with the black ribbon of the Declaration Signers; somber modernism was raising its head by then; earlier wig-ribbons were all colors of the spectrum and often several of them together.

The sons of the rich were put into wigs by the time they were nine, and sometimes at seven. Even field slaves were caught by the fashion and tied on a lock of hair with a string! This would come within the definition of a "scratch" wig, as covering only a portion of the head. Old newspaper advertisements for runaway servants occasionally describe the fugitives as wearing scratch wigs, but no identifiable picture of such an adornment has turned up.

There is no such thing as a comfortable wig, so, as soon as a gentleman found himself at home, in company where he might relax, off the pesky thing came, to be replaced by a soft cap or a turban. Some of the caps had long tassels hung to them. With the cap, it was appropriate to wear a flowered-silk dressing gown, called a "banyan," full length and blazing with color. Southern planters often rode over their own fields in their indoor caps. Visiting Englishmen criticized them severely for this and for their generally casual attire.

Women's Clothes

Modern feminine fashions seem to change radically from year to year. They changed the same way in the eighteenth century, though not quite so quickly, because they followed the whims of London and the "latest advices" had to travel by sailing ships. There were no fashion magazines. Instead, dolls, called "fashion babies," were dressed in the newest London mode and sent over, to be exhibited in the shops of Philadelphia and Boston, where they created a flurry of female excitement that spread slowly to the smaller centers.

Until 1760 women dressed their hair simply, drawing it back from the forehead, or leaving a couple of curls there and drawing the rest back

George II "fashion baby" (restored)

into a loose knot. A curled lock or two was often left free to hang on a shoulder. Indoors and out, the hair was covered by some kind of frilled cap that was likely to be so big as to forbid the wearing of a hat. At first, a "frontage," goffered like a ruff, stuck up hornlike as much as a foot from a woman's forehead. Later this calmed down and the cap grew streamers, called "lappets," that hung down on either side like the ears of a hound dog. A hood often served in place of a hat, and usually it had a cape, made as part of it, that reached the shoulders, the waist, or the ground. A hood could be put on over, or behind, a cap without doing any damage. Simpler women often tied a big kerchief, which they called a "clout," over their heads.

Soon after England was burdened with her third George, the ladies began to do things to their hair. By pulling it up over large pads, they built towers upon their heads, or rather had them built —the job had to be done by a professional. Something more than mere pinning was needed to keep hair in place on such a structure, so flour paste was liberally used. The edifice was heavily powdered

George III coiffure

Clout and hood

and was surmounted by false curls, plumes, and bunches of ribbon.

A lady who had spent money on such a masterpiece had to keep it for a while and to be very careful of it. She slept with her neck on a wooden block, so as not to disturb her tresses at night, and she allowed the coiffure to stay unopened so long that various unpleasant things happened in it, of which the appearance of weevil in the paste was not the worst. The drawbacks of this headdress finally brought women to wearing wigs.

Bodices were worn tight. They were stiffened with whalebone, or, if they were limp, they were worn over stiffened "stays." Bodices were usually open down the front to expose embroidered "stomachers."

Bare necks and chests were much in evidence, with a "modesty piece" of lace or lawn standing up across the front of the bodice. Further modesty (and warmth) could be achieved by wearing a "tippet" of gauze, cloth, or fur, depending on the season. Clear up until wartime, women's sleeves usually had turned-back cuffs, and even the simplest country girl wore some kind of white frill

showing below them. Sleeves seldom reached much below the elbow, except on riding habits.

A petticoat was still called a petticoat, even when nearly all of it was exposed to view. It was likely to be a quite heavy garment, often made of two layers of material quilted together in a pattern that was puffed up a little by stuffing the spaces between the lines of stitches with wool. A petticoat was extended on a "farthingale," a set of hoops that varied from time to time in both size and shape. Unpretentious women compromised

Mistress and maid.
The lady wears pocket hoops and a tippet

on some padding on the hips and usually wore quite short petticoats. Around 1750 "pocket hoops" were the thing. These spread the petticoat much further athwartships than fore-and-aft, producing the queenly, flattened look that is now exemplified in the hostesses' costumes at Williamsburg. Pocket hoops have an advantage in that one side, or both, may be modestly lifted for passing through a narrow door.

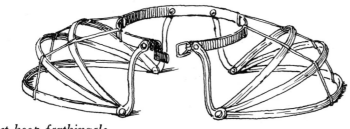

Pocket-hoop farthingale

On top of the petticoat an overskirt was tucked up in about as many ways as anyone could imagine, and there's no question but that it made a very charming appearance, though it was ill-adapted for outdoor sports. At one time, early in the century, a kind of sleeveless robe, called a "sacque" was worn. In some mysterious way this came to be blended with the overskirt, and the union produced the sack dress that persisted until after the Revolution. In mature form it had a couple of box pleats across the back at the shoulders and hung straight to the ground behind. The sack dress had its own sleeves and was joined under them to the bodice, which matched it. From the bottom of the bodice to the hem, the dress was usually, but not always, open and was draped up, or back, or both, according to fancy and fashion.

Ladies rode horses, using sidesaddles and, obviously, their hoops and sack dresses were ill-suited for such use. So a lady of quality had to have a special riding habit. It was hoopless, naturally, and made of cloth or velvet, with a skirt very long on the left side, to hang over the stirrup foot. The upper garment was a coat, made so much like a man's that Sir Roger de Coverley nearly said "Sir" to a lady. Masculine neckwear and a tricorn hat were correct with the outfit, though in the seventies somebody introduced a plumed picture hat for riding. Mr. Thomas Gainsborough could be suspected.

At the very end of the Colonial period women's shoes became extremely dainty, made of satin, with the thinnest and narrowest of soles and with slender heels a couple of inches high. But for most

A riding habit and two sack dresses

Women's footwear.
A leather shoe, and a brocade slipper in a light clog. At the right, the
clog is tilted up to show the block that kept it on by pressing against the shoe sole

of the century shoes were fairly sturdy, with good, square heels. The toes were always more pointed than was usual on a man's shoe. Leather was used for every day but party shoes were often made of brocade or embroidered silk. Some ladies still staggered around in the mud on the same kind of pattens that had served the seventeenth century, but a good many used light clogs, which were easier to walk in and which frequently were made to match the shoes they were to be worn with.

Out of doors on foot a lady met either dust or mud, and it behooved her to have her finery pretty well covered. The scarlet riding hood was efficient, and so many of them were worn that an English visitor saw them as the hallmark of American women. Another favorite outdoor coverall was the pelisse. It had full sleeves; it buttoned up to the neck; and it hung almost to the ground, all the way around. Not a thing of beauty, but it would cover almost anything. In the time of big hair-dos, a calash was worn with a pelisse. It took its name from the collapsible top of an open carriage and it, too, was collapsible. In form it was a segment of a sphere, in size, half as big as a washtub.

Of accessories we have space to say but little, and of materials, less. Ladies carried fans no matter what the temperature. They carried muffs in winter and wore long gloves and lace mitts, either of which might be tied around the arm at the top or buttoned to the cuff. Masks were worn outdoors to protect the complexion. Some were merely held in the hand. Another kind had a silver mouthpiece, on which the wearer might clamp her pretty teeth, if she still had them. Still a third mask was provided with two short silk strings, each with a bead on its end; these, too, were held in the mouth and they *permitted talking*. Masks were made of

stiffened velvet, or of silk, black, white, or green.

Another oddity worn by ladies was the "etwee" (etui), or "equipage," a small silver or morocco case, hung from the bodice on a "stayhook." The etwee contained a nail file, scissors, earpick, toothpick, and tweezers. Sometimes a stayhook was used to support a "bosom bottle," with a little water in it to keep a nosegay fresh.

Ready for travel, in pelisse, mask, and calash.
The lady's trunk is covered with deer hide, with the hair left on

Poise

"Pudding"

Youth

Great stress was put upon an erect carriage in woman, and little girls were systematically tortured to achieve it. They sat for a couple of hours every day strapped to boards to make their backs flat; they wore sheet metal and wooden stays to keep their waists slim, and also stays with needles built into them to prick tired little skins that dared to relax for an instant. Girls were made to walk about balancing objects on their heads, to give them poise. There were people to whom this was the sole purpose of a book.

In the first sixty years or so of the eighteenth century, when a child came out of petticoats, at six, he (or she) went directly into the complete costume of an adult. This seems to have remained true of girls for the whole century. Little girls with rich parents wore all the panoply of their mothers,

including hoops, stays, and masks. But, in the last quarter, boys had an intermediate uniform, a long-sleeved one-piece suit worn over a linen shirt, that bridged the gap of a couple of years between dresses and yellow nankeen breeches. The suit was curious in that the jacket and pants were continuous in the rear, but the front flap of the breeches was fastened to the jacket by a row of buttons across the chest.

Toddlers still wore hanging sleeves until 1750 or thereabouts; after that they had leading strings, attached to a belt. By means of these an adult could restore lost balance. Busy mothers who had no servant to watch a child would encase it in a "pudding" and let it fend for itself. A pudding was a soft bolster, tied around a child's middle and suspended from its shoulders by tapes, somewhat in the manner of a cork life jacket. Wearing one, a baby might toddle and topple with impunity.

Pewter nursing bottle

Top whipping

Diversions

Though the children wore the clothes of adults, it isn't intended to suggest that they were always dressed up and sitting decorously about, like little ladies and gentlemen. Girls have to have dolls. If an imported one with a wooden body and bisque head and hands wasn't to be had, little Miss made shift to love a baby home-produced from cornhusks. The daughters of "quality" were somewhat restricted in the things they might do for amusement, but country girls could join, wholeheartedly and loudly, in their brothers' game of tag or blindman's buff.

Boys pitched horseshoes, shot marbles, and, if they had any pennies, they pitched pennies, calling the game "huzzlecap." Boys also whipped tops, prolonging the initial spin by stroking the top with a whiplash. This required at least as much skill as the manipulation of a yo-yo. There has always been some kind of ball game. With Colonial boys it was stoolball. It seems to have had some relation to cricket; in fact, a three-legged stool was known as a cricket, and in this game a ball was bowled at such a stool, which was defended by a batter.

Men found outdoor diversions, too, though more often in the form of sport than in games. The exception was bowls. Every village had its green, down the length of which teams rolled their bowls, earnestly trying to group them as closely as possible around a single white ball, called the "jack," placed near the opposite end of the green. Reaching the jack was complicated by the bowls being slightly egg-shaped rather than perfectly spherical. This wasn't accidental; it was a deliberate hazard. The game is still popular in England.

Fox hunting, in the traditional way, with horse and hound, engaged the gentry of the South; up North they tended to shoot the varmints. Horse racing was popular everywhere, though in some parts actual participation was restricted by law to gentlemen. Races were run, either across country from point to point, regardless of terrain or obstacles, or they were run as straightaways, on a flat marked course. The wide mile-long Duke of Gloucester Street in Williamsburg made a perfect racecourse. Other towns, less happily laid out, ran their races in near-by fields.

As they still are, races were often run in connection with a fair. There were fairs in most centers at least once a year. They provided an opportunity for local trading and for buying small luxuries, as well as an excuse for athletic contests and competitions in music and dancing. Catching a greased pig was a favorite feature, so was climbing a greased pole. Both of these events were messy, and correspondingly hilarious to watch. On the artistic side, surely the occasion at Westover has seldom been equaled; there twenty fiddlers played in unison—each a different tune!

Fairs also featured foot races, wrestling, and bouts at cudgels straight out of Robin Hood. Such things as silver shoe buckles were given as prizes. Shoes were the prize for dancing. In a singing contest the contenders were given "liquor sufficient to clear their windpipes." In fact, everybody was given liquor. Whenever there was a celebration,

as on the King's birthday, a town treasury was likely to pay for a keg of rum, to be consumed by all comers; or the Royal Governor might make a gift of such a keg, to entertain the common people while the gentry were getting tight on brandy. Special occasions of this sort were usually the excuse for an "illumination." Bonfires were built in the streets at night, and every window in town had a candle in it. There was an illumination in Philadelphia to celebrate the surrender of Cornwallis at Yorktown.

A public celebration also furnished an excuse for a ball. It was held in a mansion or in the ballroom of a large inn. Such an affair was attended

The "Sir Roger de Coverley," early in the century

Bar of an inn about 1760

only by the "right people." They were good at dancing. English visitors reported, with blank astonishment, that these crude provincials danced as well as the best London society. It isn't surprising, for they certainly worked at it. There were dancing schools in every town, even in staid Boston. In the South, itinerant dancing masters worked the plantation circuit. While they were present, the owner, his wife, and their children ceased all other activity and took lessons. They danced all morning, all afternoon, and far into the night.

A slave playing a fiddle sufficed as music for such practice work, but for a big party there would be a couple of fiddles, a cello, and a flute, with a harpsichord too, if one was available. All dancing was not as sedate as the formal Minuet. Many of the dances were violently active. The "Square Dance" was popular under the name of "Contra Dance" or "Country Dance," and so was the romping "Sir Roger de Coverley" that we call the "Virginia Reel." Jigs and Hornpipes were danced at balls by ladies in hoops and gentlemen in powdered wigs.

The ladies and gentlemen sometimes had an opportunity to see a play. By 1750 professional acting companies were touring under travel conditions that make any more recent barnstorming look like de luxe touring. Common folk could take in puppet shows. To people who saw no other kind of drama, Punch and Judy was a kind of miracle, utterly real and tensely exciting, a subject for a year's conversation, with the dialogue recalled almost verbatim.

Inns

In addition to its role as hostelry, the eighteenth-century inn was a local club. For the cost of an occasional penny for a quart of beer, a man might hear the latest news, listen in on the discussions of the best minds in the neighborhood, or amuse himself at the game of his choice. The gentlemen played cards or backgammon. The laborer played draughts (which was checkers), or skittles, or shuffleboard. Skittles was played in a covered alley and was the ancestor of tenpins. The pins were called skittles, and the object was to knock them over with a lopsided ball a foot in diameter.

In the warm bar of an inn, on a chilly night, a man could buy not only a tot of rum or a pot of hot mulled ale, he could also get a little tobacco to smoke along with it and could pick up a pipe from the public rack. These clay pipes, called "church-wardens," had stems fourteen inches long. It was customary to break off an inch or so of stem before lighting one, to give yourself a fresh mouthpiece. Though hundreds of pipe bowls have been found on Colonial archaeological sites, none of them ever has its long stem. In case you are wondering how a small hole was put through a fourteen-inch clay stem, the stem was molded around a straw that burnt away when the pipe was fired in the kiln.

Mention has been made of the ritual snuff-sniffing of the gentry. Many of them felt that snuff, to be at its best, should be freshly ground, so they ground their own. The commonalty also took snuff, but they didn't sniff it; they "dipped" it or "rubbed" it. A sturdy plowman would pull out his underlip with his left thumb and forefinger and fill the space between lip and gum with a generous dip of snuff. Then he would take a chewed stick from his pocket and use it to massage his gums thoroughly with snuff. This way of indulgence was by no means confined to males, and it is by no means extinct among the men and women who still take snuff.

Snuffbox

New England meetinghouse

152

Churches

Church attendance was compulsory in nearly all the Colonies, but there were few people who *wanted* to stay away. Quite aside from its spiritual purpose, the church was the community source of mental stimulus, of drama, of gossip, and of news. A couple of hours of theological hairsplitting was endured as a necessary mortification of the flesh. The solid citizen who lapsed into slumber had nothing worse to fear than having his ear tickled, first by a fur-tipped rod in the hands of the tithing man or the verger, and again by a pointed sarcasm from the pulpit.

In New England the unadorned meetinghouse first acquired a coat of white paint, outside, to protect the wood, then inside also. The belfry on the roof moved over and became a bell tower, made lovely with moldings and spire. Its base formed a vestibule and sometimes housed the stairs that led to the side galleries, added to increase seating capacity. Presently, the posts that held the galleries up became classic columns and the interior, though still severely plain, was beautiful. Happily, many of the meetinghouses still stand; there is hardly an old New England town that lacks one.

The earliest Southern church buildings were Gothic in style, not as imitations, but because the

153

builders knew no other way to build them. They were brick, with walls a couple of feet thick, and when the style changed at the end of the seventeenth century both the bulk and the material were carried over. The newer churches had painted wooden bell towers, set on brick bases, but the Southern version was a little "fatter" than the New England tower. The nave windows were high and round-topped, with sliding wooden sash that could be opened on warm days. Surrounding every church was the burying ground, with its flat-topped tombs enclosed by a brick wall.

Inside the Southern church there were galleries across the rear wall and transepts, occupied by servants and slaves. The pews of the congregation were high-walled wooden pens, affording privacy to the occupants and commonly fitted out according to the personal taste of the owner. Important people, like governors, often had curtained pews, to make them invisible to the common herd. In order to see and be seen, as well as heard, the parson delivered his sermon from a boxlike pulpit set high on a pedestal and reached by a small flight of steps. Above his head was a wooden canopy, for a sounding board.

In the South the vestry of the parish was the governing body not only of the church but of the community also. It was responsible for the upkeep of roads, for the registry of earmarks denoting the ownership of cattle, and for the care of paupers. A parish pauper was required to wear an identifying metal badge sewn on his sleeve. In most cases the wearers of these lived with some family, whom the parish paid. In New England, roads and paupers were the responsibility of the town meeting, which, though it had its origin in the church, came to operate on its own. Only landowners and church members, persons "with a stake in the Colony," still had the right to vote, but a petition of *any* ten men could call a meeting, and anyone might stand up in it to state his opinions.

Prison

It occurred to no one in the eighteenth century that a prison should have any quality other than

A felon's cell in a Colonial "gaol"

strength. If you could keep a prisoner where you put him, his comfort and health needed no consideration. A Colonial prison cell usually had one barred window, small and high. A bundle of straw was provided as a bed, and the only thing in the way of a seat was the commode. If a prisoner was at all aggressive, he was kept in irons. Food was passed to him through a slot. Only if he was specially favored was he allowed a few minutes now and then to walk in the walled gaolyard.

It wasn't until the eighteenth century that slaves became numerous enough to suggest the frightening possibility of a rebellion. This fear brought about the enactment of harsh laws for slave control. No slave could appear on the streets after dark without a pass from his master, and no slave could visit, or entertain, after sunset. Since he had worked all of the daylight hours, this restricted his social life to Sunday. The law "protected" slaves by limiting their working hours to fifteen a day. A slave could own no dogs, because they encouraged surreptitious coon hunting, and the hunters showed up tired for work. It was the conviction of slave owners that all Negroes were born tired, which is in no way surprising.

The masters of slaves were haunted by the thought of poison, so any slave who gave medicine to anyone could be hanged. The harshest punishment was reserved for the slave who murdered his master. Hanging wasn't severe enough; he was burned at the stake. And, lest you think this was only in the South, it occurred in nearly every Colony, and as late as 1775.

On the other hand, it should be remembered that the Colonials tried to stop the slave trade. Virginia and South Carolina petitioned the king of England time and again to stop it but it was too lucrative and he always refused. Thomas Jefferson's first draft of the Declaration of Independence contained an impassioned indictment of slavery, which Congress struck out of the final document.

Sickness and Medicine

Human health and sanitary conditions weren't noticeably better in the eighteenth century than they had been in the seventeenth. Death, especially the death of young children, was commonplace. It dominated people's thoughts, and they went in for extremely morose sentimentality.

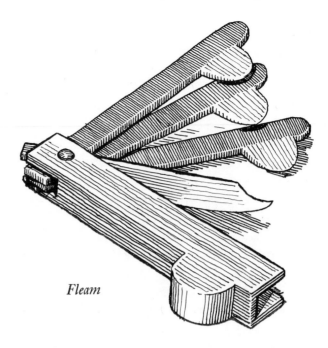

Fleam

The science of medicine was beginning to come out of the witchcraft era; men studied it seriously, but the best of them were almost totally ignorant by today's standards. The mainstay of professional medicine was phlebotomy, which was opening a vein and letting the patient bleed into a basin to see if it would do him any good. The operation was performed with an unsterile instrument called a fleam. It might be done to treat pneumonia, malaria, or an upset stomach. Blistering the skin, to treat internal disorders, was in high favor. Violent purges and other weird potions were administered, and the stronger patients survived them. Almost everybody took a day off once every month or so to "take physic," whether he needed it or not. The less said of surgery, the pleasanter.

Yellow fever, smallpox, and cholera struck repeatedly in all the larger centers. Brave doctors and volunteer nurses did what they could, but, being ignorant of even the causes of the diseases, they might almost as well have run away with the rest of the population. Vaccination against smallpox was known and crudely practiced, but most people would have nothing to do with it.

Learning

A medical school was started in Philadelphia in mid-century, and other sciences began to receive attention. John Bartram, the Quaker botanist, corresponded with Linnaeus in Sweden and was the discoverer and classifier of many American plants. Benjamin Franklin was a fellow of the Royal Society and was famous all over Europe long before he won laurels as a diplomat. Learning generally was in good favor. There were half a dozen reputable colleges in the Colonies.

For ordinary schooling there were some public schools, though attendance at them was neither compulsory, general, nor constant. The beginner still learned his letters from the hornbook, or its country cousin, the battledore, which lacked the protective horn. He then progressed to the *New England Primer,* used everywhere, and to Dilworth's "Speller." Spelling continued to be largely an original art, even among well-educated people. Dr. Samuel Johnson's *Dictionary* was the great fixative of English spelling, but it wasn't published until 1755 and had but slight effect on this side of the water for a long time after that. Much time was given to penmanship; the possession of "a legible, joyning hand, plain to be read" was considered the mark of an educated man.

The sons of the rich continued to be sent to England for their final education and sometimes for nearly all of it; but it was possible for a man to get a sound education in the Colonies. One wonders if there is significance in the fact that the ringleaders of the Revolution who thrust their necks into the noose for Independence and who were also the leaders in welding the nation—Jefferson, Hamilton, Madison, Franklin, both Adamses, and George Washington—were all educated in America.

Officially the Colonial period ended on the Fourth of July, 1776; but it had really ended quite a while before that. It was over when ordinary people began to sense that all thirteen Colonies had the same problems. They ceased being British before they themselves realized what had happened; and the whole meaning of their lives was different from then on. The ways of life began to change too, slowly, but far faster and in different directions than if the Americans had remained loyal to the Crown.

Schoolroom

ABOUT THE AUTHOR

Edwin Tunis has a distinguished reputation as an artist, illustrator, and muralist. His articles have appeared in various magazines and he has exhibited at the Baltimore Museum of Art, Society of American Etchers, National Academy of Design, Victoria and Albert Museum, and many other galleries. His most ambitious art project was a mural depicting the History of Spices, which is 145 feet long and took two and a half years to paint.

The study of American history was always one of Mr. Tunis' passions, and it was natural for him to combine this interest with his art to produce the superb books of American social history for which he is famous. Among these are *Frontier Living,* which was first runner-up for the Newbery Medal; *Colonial Living,* which won the Thomas A. Edison Award; *Oars, Sails and Steam,* which was chosen by the A.I.G.A. as one of the "Fifty Books of the Year"; *Wheels,* which won the Gold Medal of the Boy's Clubs of America; and *The Young United States: 1783-1830,* which was nominated for the National Book Award in 1970.

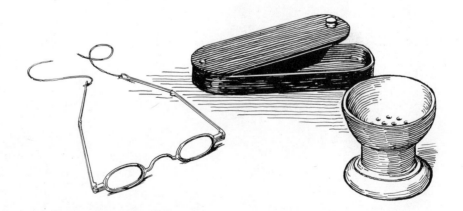

Spectacles and their case and a sand shaker for blotting ink: eighteenth century